Praise for *Welcome to the Revolution*

Brian strips off all the pious, churchy language and practices that are sometimes associated with following Christ and gives us a raw, gutsy, life-giving understanding of how to enter into a revolutionary way of life in God's Kingdom. Excellent for every Christian—new or road-worn.

—**JOHN BURKE**, Author of *No Perfect People Allowed*
and *Soul Revolution*

I don't know anyone who is better than Brian Tome at translating the Gospel into the language of unchurched, nonreligious, postmodern people. Combining personal stories with humor and insight, Brian has given us a practical, compelling, first-rate introduction to the Kingdom revolution. *Welcome to the Revolution* is the first book all new believers should read.

—**DR. GREG BOYD**, Senior Pastor, Woodland Hills Church,
Author of *Letters from a Skeptic* and *Lord or Legend?*

It has been an incredible joy to walk alongside Brian Tome as he leads the people of Crossroads into the work of justice with IJM. The passion, faith, and excitement that I've seen in Brian through this great adventure are just as evident in this marvelous guide he has written for those taking their first steps in the exhilarating journey of faith.

—**GARY A. HAUGEN**, President & CEO, International Justice Mission

Brian Tome got tired of trying to find a book about how to go from being un-churched and unfamiliar with all things "Christian," to being a follower of Christ. So he wrote the book he couldn't find—a book that could help a person transition from seeking God to knowing and growing with God. What a wonderful gift to those just starting out on their spiritual journey.

—**JOHN C. MAXWELL**, Author of *The 21 Irrefutable Laws of Leadership*

We need this kind of writing. It's simple in its style, profound in its message. It makes it possible for the new Christian to get a handle on what it means to be a follower of Christ in a time when there is much confusion as to what that is all about.

—**TONY CAMPOLO**, PhD, Eastern University

WELCOME TO THE
REVOLUTION

A FIELD GUIDE FOR NEW BELIEVERS

BRIAN TOME

THOMAS NELSON
Since 1798

NASHVILLE   DALLAS   MEXICO CITY   RIO DE JANEIRO   BEIJING

Published in Nashville, Tennessee, by Thomas Nelson. Thomas Nelson is a registered trademark of Thomas Nelson, Inc.

Thomas Nelson, Inc. titles may be purchased in bulk for educational, business, fund-raising, or sales promotional use. For information, please e-mail SpecialMarkets@ThomasNelson.com.

Unless otherwise noted, Scripture quotations are taken from the HOLY BIBLE: NEW INTERNATIONAL VERSION®. © 1973, 1978, 1984 by International Bible Society. Used by permission of Zondervan Publishing House. All rights reserved.

Library of Congress Cataloging-in-Publication Data

Tome, Brian.
  Welcome to the revolution : a field guide for new believers / by Brian Tome.
    p. cm.
  ISBN 978-0-8499-2005-9 (trade paper)
  1. Christian life. I. Title.
BV4501.3.T654 2008
248.4—dc22   2008012215

Printed in the United States of America

08 09 10 11 12 RRD 5 4 3 2 1

ACKNOWLEDGMENTS

LIBBY TOME: You are not only beautiful, but you are the backbone to my life. People can see beauty but they can't see a backbone. Yet without it, we wouldn't go anywhere. You are a significant part of everything God does in my life. It is an honor being in the Kingdom with you. Thank you for your sacrifices.

LENA TOME: You are a light to everyone who knows you. Your light is revealing and strong. I've learned things about myself as a result of that strength. I count you as my sister in Christ more than I do my physical daughter. Thank you for your endurance.

JAKE TOME: I'll spend more time with you than any other man on the earth. We are truly blood brothers, which makes me happy and proud. You have a heart after God that I wish I had at your age. Thank you for your resilience and modeling for me what strong kindness looks like.

MORIAH TOME: Your joy is infectious. Seeing how you dance, bounce and tumble helps me to better understand the lighthearted side of God. You are made in His image, and I aspire to have your countenance. Thanks for being one of a kind.

Dave, Art, Frank, Brad, Bob, Michael, and the dozens of other guys who I've seen take their first steps in the Revolution of the Kingdom of God: You not only inspire me as brothers, but you've been a great test market for the concepts in the book. Thank you for allowing me to be a normal guy.

Matt Baugher and the Thomas Nelson Team: Thanks for believing in this project and helping it get out to more people to move the Kingdom forward.

Jonathan Rogers: Your writing insights and organizing ability have made a huge difference. Thank you.

Darin Yates: You helped bring me emotional freedom when I was wounded. You then helped bring me organizational freedom, which created space to get this book done. Thanks for being a warrior.

Liz Young: Without you on staff and as a friend, this book wouldn't have happened. Or, if it did, the quality wouldn't be as high. Thanks for bringing your giftedness to bear in a tight turn-around time.

Crossroads: I hope this book represents all of your sacrifices well. You are the greatest group of revolutionaries I've ever done life with. Thank you.

Welcome to the Revolution!

CONTENTS

NOWHERE TO TURN

The most important thing I had to do on my first day in Cincinnati was find a gym so I could play basketball at lunch, and I lucked out on the first try. The Cincinnati Athletic Club is full of guys who work for a living—which means they don't have much to prove on the court. It also means they aren't that good. That's good, because I'm not that good either. Sure, every once in a while my teeth get hung up on the net, but for the most part my game doesn't cause much of a stir.

But there is something else that does cause a stir: when guys find out what I do for a living. The thing is, I like being a guy—a normal guy. I like normal guy things, and I do normal guy things like drink a beer on my back porch and scratch myself when no one's looking. (Ladies, most of us do that. Including the guy you're dating.) But when another guy finds out I'm a pastor, it seems like it gets really difficult for him to relate to me . . . unless he sees me scratch myself.

So I've learned over the years that when making new guy acquaintances, I've got to be very intentional. I need to get to know people before I ask the question, "What do you do for a living?" Because as soon as I ask, they'll return the question. And when I answer, "I'm a pastor," all hell breaks loose. I see it in their eyes. First, they do a rewind of all the jokes they've told and all the after-the-missed-shot cussing. Then they give a dazed and quizzical look, which is usually followed by something like, "You're full of . . . (pause, reconsider) . . . crap."

The average guy—and the average woman, for that matter—doesn't have much real-world experience with a friend who believes passionately in Jesus, who reads the Bible and prays regularly and actually claims to hear from God. Many of us don't know someone who believes he's part of a community that's literally changing the world. And not a sideline kind of change or something that he's committed to just on Sundays when others are watching. But I'm talking about people who know it's a total commitment and believe that God can get a hold of your life and radically change you, while you change the world.

Art was the first guy on the court who learned the truth about what I do. We were eating lunch when he popped the question, and it took me half the lunchtime to convince him I wasn't lying. Then came Dave, Frank, and before I knew it, my nickname was "Preach," and the guys began to see transformation in their lives. They weren't changing just because I was hanging around, but because they sensed God's truth, and they began pursuing it. They started spending money differently, praying for things they used to leave to chance, staying faithful in their marriages, reading the Bible and actually doing what it says. Big stuff. Life-changing stuff.

For many of us, our gut is saying there's more in this life than what we currently understand, and we just haven't found it yet. We've sat through masses or church services that didn't speak to our hearts. We've watched people suffer and then questioned the power of God. We've never heard the real and thorough message of Jesus, so we've dismissed the "Christian" life. Or maybe we've felt the pull of God, but it freaked us out, so we resisted and kept our eyes on the ground.

I've seen that kind of resistance to God. I've had people like Misha come talk to me. This young woman was intrigued, confused, and bothered. She felt God starting to move in her life, and she wasn't happy about it. She was afraid of being sucked in, and she didn't want to be "religious" like the people she'd grown to despise, or at least disrespect. She had a list of complaints about Christianity: sexism, elitism, prejudice, hypocrisy.

But during the months Misha had been spending time in our church community, her defenses started to break down. For the first time she saw Christ-followers being real with one another and trying hard to apply the Bible to their lives because they are so inspired and excited about it. She discovered they weren't all checking their brains at the door. They were being real; they weren't all capital-H Hypocrites.

So Misha came to find me. She was still ready to unload all the standard objections and make her point that Christ-following just wasn't for her. You might say it was a last-ditch effort to resist God moving in her life. I call it last-ditch because even as Misha was voicing her objections, she was also revealing a nagging inner sense that something wasn't right. And it wouldn't be right until she had this Jesus thing figured out.

To Misha's dismay—and, in the end, her joy—the things we talked about that day clicked. "Don't worry right now about what God does with the person who lives in India and never hears about Jesus," I said. "Worry about yourself. You know Jesus brought an overwhelming message of love—that He lived on Earth, died for us, and impacted this world. And you know you can receive His love. Is there any reason why you don't want that right now?"

"No, there isn't," Misha answered, her hands trembling, tears falling. And then God did what mere human powers of persuasion can't. His power broke completely through to her confused and seeking heart.

"Talk to God," I said. "Tell Him you're thankful for what He's already been doing in your life. Tell Him you want to be forgiven for blowing Him off, for offending Him. Ask Him to come into your life, and the Holy Spirit will enter your being. Misha, He'll mark you as one of His. No matter how rough or awkwardly you say it, God knows what you're getting at, and He will respond." And right then Misha chose to pray.

Misha stepped into a brand-new life in Jesus. That's how Paul, an early follower of Jesus, described it in Romans 6:23—a new life in Jesus Christ. It's not just making a few tweaks, not adhering to a few new rules or learning a new vocabulary. It's like being set down in a strange land where the whole landscape is different.

But Misha didn't have a close friend who could be her field guide for this new journey. She didn't have any understanding of God's Kingdom or even a frame of reference for how to read the Bible and grow in her understanding of God. Yet Misha had to make the transition from seeking God to growing and walking with Him. She needed help that would go beyond a large gathering with a band and a speaker.

I knew she was a reader, so I thought, *No problem. I'll go to my bookshelf and pull out one of the many books that can get her started in this new life.* But as I looked around, I was surprised that nothing leaped off the shelves.

When I help people in the midst of an addiction, it's obvious which books they should read. When I help people wrestle through the headier issues of Christianity, books abound. If you have a leadership issue or a relational issue, my library has the answers. But a book about how to go from being "unchurched"—unfamiliar with Christian jargon, the Christian story, the Christian "subculture"—to being a follower of Christ? Nothing.

That's why I've written this book. Because there are a lot of Mishas out there: people who need to know the essentials of the Christ-following life as well as what it means to live those out and have an exciting, ever-deepening relationship with Jesus. I'm writing this book for people like the guys at my gym: people who've never been fully exposed to the real Jesus but feel compelled to understand Him, and who want straight talk, not Christianese—not clichéd spiritual language that doesn't reach them or seems irrelevant, inauthentic, and narrow. And I'm writing for people who want to run toward something, believe in something, fight for something.

Do you know what I love about the Mishas of the world? They understand that following Jesus transforms you. That's something you might forget if you spend too much time among the "Biblically Correct." If you're a follower of Jesus, you haven't just joined a club, signed on to a set of beliefs, or learned a secret handshake. Jesus will turn your life upside down. But there's more than that. He's all about turning the rest of the world upside down too.

Does all this sound crazy? That doesn't bother me a bit. I wrote this book for people like you. Something has happened or is happening inside you and around you, and you can't fully explain it. You are left to conclude that it must be God. And yet there are a whole host of things that Christians are "supposed" to believe that you are unsure of—or maybe that you don't believe at all.

You don't believe that God created the world in six literal days six thousand years ago? Fine. You're uneasy about the idea that

Jesus never committed a sin? Okay, whatever. You don't want to start looking like a televangelist? Me neither.

You've entered into a journey. You don't have to believe and do everything right now. In fact, there are things that you and other followers of Jesus believe and live out that might later be repudiated. It's all part of the full and surprising adventure of being in relationship with God. It's what makes God's Kingdom different from any other.

So welcome to a new life. Welcome to the Revolution.

THE REVOLUTION OF THE KINGDOM OF GOD

Jesus didn't come to start a new religion. He came to start a revolution. He brought a passionate message of change—radical, all-encompassing change—to a world in which every part of life was infiltrated by chaos, despair, pain, and isolation. He brought love.

Jesus wasn't content to give people a new belief system to replace their old one. That stuff doesn't reach the heart; it just layers on rules, breeds guilt, and causes people to rebel because they can't keep up with it or they realize it's all for show. Jesus brought the opposite: an entirely new way to live, a system of totality—and the system the world was initially designed to follow. A system not driven by an iron fist or laws or prestige, but by the transforming power of love.

The Kingdom of God isn't something dreamed up by religious professionals. In the New Testament section of the Bible—the books written shortly after the life of Jesus—the phrases "Kingdom of God" and "Kingdom of heaven" (they're used interchangeably) occur over 150 times. And when Jesus speaks to a huge crowd, in what's known as "The Sermon on the Mount," He explains how to pray, and that prayer asks for God's Kingdom to be brought to earth just as it exists in heaven.[1] What does that mean to you and me today? God is telling us to bring the Kingdom here, and to bring it *now*.

No wonder this requires a revolution.

But let me back up a little and give some historical context—and it won't be as bad as it sounds, I promise. This is actually pretty interesting history.

Palestine, where Jesus lived and died, was an outpost of the Roman Empire. The local population—mostly Jewish—was ruled by foreign oppressors: the Romans. The Romans had incredible power, cunning, and influence. They conquered and ruled with violence. So, as you might imagine, most of the Jews in Palestine hated the Romans, because, basically, the Jews had become Roman slaves. And to top it off, the Romans worshipped false gods—including the Roman emperor himself. This was a huge offense to the Jews, who believed in only one God. You can see why the Jews were looking for a way out.

Sin: the use of our freedom to have any attitude, thought, or action that dishonors God. Also, the use of our freedom not to choose an attitude, thought, or action that would honor God. Until we have a relationship with Jesus, we are in a state of sin.

---

1. Matthew 6:10

The Jews had long prayed and hoped for someone to deliver them—to save them. God had promised, after all, to send someone who would set them free. They called this deliverer "the Messiah," and they all thought they knew what to expect: he would lead a rebellion against the Romans, crush the oppressors, and then rule over his people as a mighty yet benevolent leader.

So when John the Baptist (a Paul Revere-type prophet who had earned the respect of the Jews even though he ate bugs and honey) came out from the woods shouting, "Repent, because the kingdom of heaven is at hand!" people noticed. They held their breath. "He who is coming after me is mightier than me," John said, and the Jews, longing for rescue, thought, *That's what I'm talking about! Bring it on! I need to get me some Messiah.*

And Jesus was the Messiah; He just wasn't the Messiah the Jews were expecting. He came to deliver them from oppression, but that deliverance didn't look the way they thought it would. Jesus brought a Revolution all right, but His Revolution was much more all-encompassing than a mere political upheaval or battlefield slaughter. It was more than just freedom from a cruel government. It was freedom from a selfish and unfulfilling way of life. In other words, it was freedom from sin.

THE STORY OF MATTHEW, a Jewish tax collector, is one of my favorite stories about how one man rocked the Revolution and lived out the Kingdom. First, let me explain what it meant to be a tax collector in Jesus' time, so you know what a strange beginning Matthew's journey had. These guys weren't IRS agents. Even if IRS agents aren't the most popular guys around, they're at least respectable. You don't cross to the other side of the street when you

Disciples: friends of Jesus who decided to learn from His life and live as He lived.

see the tax man coming. But in Jesus' day, tax collectors were the lowest of the low. It wasn't only that they'd hang around your front porch and then just happen to run into you during your morning jog and remind you that you owed them. They were considered unclean, meaning they couldn't worship with, eat with, or have voluntary contact with other Jews. Why were tax collectors so hated? Because they were collaborators with the Romans. The Romans gave tax collectors a quota, a minimum to collect, but they were free to overcharge and pocket the excess. In other words, they had a well-earned reputation as self-serving traitors.

So picture this: Jesus had already gathered up six disciples—mostly blue-collar guys, fishermen. Then one afternoon as they were walking through town, Jesus noticed a man in the tax office—and that was Matthew. Jesus stopped, looked into the office, and said two words to him: "Follow Me." And I love Matthew's reaction: "He left everything behind, and rose and began to follow Him".[2]

Matthew left everything behind. He began to follow.

Jesus was calling Matthew out of the Roman world. In that world, Matthew was an oppressor, a sellout. Family love, patriotism, the respect of his neighbors, common decency—all of that was trumped by Matthew's love of money and power. You could hardly invent a better example of a person who sold out to the ways of the world.

---

2 . Mark 2:14, paraphrase

But I should point out that Matthew was also a victim. Can you imagine how trapped he felt? He must have hated himself. And yet he couldn't quit. First, there would have been some risk in telling the Roman Empire to kiss off. And second—probably more important—how would he support himself if he quit? Was he supposed to go get a job with one of the neighbors he'd been ripping off?

Imagine the relief Matthew felt when Jesus said, "Follow Me." Jesus was saying, in effect, "Leave all this behind. You don't have to live like this. I know it sounds radical, maybe impossible, but I've got something better for you." Matthew didn't even hesitate. He immediately saw the power of God and said, "I want in on that. Let's go."

Matthew was so pumped about this new life that he threw a party. He invited all his friends to come hang out with Jesus. He wanted them to get a taste of what he had just begun to experience. And who do you expect the friends of a tax collector would be? Other tax collectors and sinners, of course. Certainly not "polite society." Yet Jesus went to the party, and He took along His other disciples. They ate with people whom no good Jew would be caught dead with.

> **Ways of the World / the World:** a pattern or system that plays itself out on earth, but is contrary to the law and love of God.

The religious professionals were scandalized. They rolled their eyes to heaven and wagged their self-righteous fingers, because they had no idea what it meant to love.

Here's the irony of Matthew's story, and here's why I like it so much. The Kingdom of God was a more obvious threat to the religious establishment than it was to the political establishment. Did Jesus come to overthrow the "Roman" way of doing things? Yes. Absolutely yes. But that doesn't mean He came to put the religious establishment on top and in its place. Jesus was leading a revolution against the religious professionals' system too. He showed that the powerful would not stay powerful, and the weak would not stay weak.

> **Kingdom of God:** a holistic movement or force pushed by God, in line with His law and His love.

And guess what happened to Matthew, the old tax collector, the outcast, the thief? He wrote the first account of Jesus' life, and that's the first book in the New Testament of the Bible. Because just as Matthew's life was revolutionized, he knew he could help others see the big picture of the ever-advancing Kingdom.

This is how Matthew's book starts:

A record of the genealogy of Jesus Christ the son of David, the son of Abraham: Abraham was the father of Isaac, Isaac the father of Jacob, Jacob the father of Judah and his brothers, Judah the father of Perez and Zerah, whose mother was Tamar, Perez the father of Hezron, Hezron the father of Ram, Ram the father of Amminadab, Amminadab the father of Nahshon, Nahshon the father of Salmon, Salmon the father of Boaz, whose mother was Rahab, Boaz the father of Obed, whose mother was Ruth, Obed the father of Jesse, and Jesse the father of King David.

David was the father of Solomon, whose mother had been

Uriah's wife, Solomon the father of Rehoboam, Rehoboam the father of Abijah, Abijah the father of Asa, Asa the father of Jehoshaphat, Jehoshaphat the father of Jehoram, Jehoram the father of Uzziah, Uzziah the father of Jotham, Jotham the father of Ahaz, Ahaz the father of Hezekiah, Hezekiah the father of Manasseh, Manasseh the father of Amon, Amon the father of Josiah, and Josiah the father of Jeconiah and his brothers at the time of the exile to Babylon.

After the exile to Babylon: Jeconiah was the father of Shealtiel, Shealtiel the father of Zerubbabel, Zerubbabel the father of Abiud, Abiud the father of Eliakim, Eliakim the father of Azor, Azor the father of Zadok, Zadok the father of Akim, Akim the father of Eliud, Eliud the father of Eleazar, Eleazar the father of Matthan, Matthan the father of Jacob, and Jacob the father of Joseph, the husband of Mary, of whom was born Jesus, who is called Christ.[3]

If you just read every name in that list, you're pretty impressive. (Or pretty anal.) Why did Matthew trot out this many names? Is it the old tax man, the detail jockey, coming back to haunt us?

Actually, Matthew told an interesting story with this boring list. He was giving Jesus' revolutionary credentials. From Abraham—who, like Matthew himself, was called to leave behind everything he knew—through David, Israel's greatest human king and deliverer, and through Mary, the pregnant virgin teenager, the entire sweep of history was leading to this moment of Revolution.

But it's not the "great ones" in Jesus' genealogy that I find most interesting. I wonder if Matthew, the great sinner, smiled as he recorded the other sinners and victims and losers in Jesus'

---

3. Matthew 1:1–16

family tree. For instance, Rahab, the prostitute who sold out her countrymen. Tamar, who was raped by her own brother. Solomon, who was blessed with great wisdom but traded it in due to his sexual appetite for concubines and multiple wives from different countries and religions. Even King David was an adulterer and murderer. Abraham was a liar and occasionally a coward.

I'm just saying that God had a plan from the beginning to bring about a Revolution in the most unusual ways—ways you would never imagine, and through people you'd never imagine. And, yes, that's how it still happens.

THE AMAZING THING ABOUT this Revolution Jesus started is that it's still going on. It's still growing, gobbling up more and more territory all the time. I know it might not look that way here in America. It looks like the Kingdom of God is losing ground. Porn is increasing. Church attendance is decreasing. But in the rest of the world, there are visible signs that the Kingdom of God is growing like crazy.

You may have heard that Islam is the fastest growing religion in the world. Not true. In his book *The Next Christendom: The Coming of Global Christianity*, Philip Jenkins shows that when you look at the entire world, the big story is "Southern Christianity"—that is, Christianity in the "developing" nations of Africa, Central and South America, and Asia. If current trends continue, by 2050 there will be five nations besides the United States with 100 million or more Christians: Brazil, Mexico, the Philippines, Nigeria, and the Congo.

So if it looks to "religious" American Christians as if the Kingdom of God is losing ground, maybe it's because we're still trying to work an irrelevant religious system here in America. Religion and the Kingdom of God aren't the same thing, by the way. Not even close. I define religion as any system that says, "Do this and don't do that in order to please God and find satisfaction." People in that kind of system might know the official beliefs of Christianity, but either they don't really know Jesus or they're blinded to His power—not in spite of their religious beliefs, but because of them.

When people find religion, they tend to act like they have all the answers and no doubts. I certainly fell prey to this when I found religion. My parents were taking me home from a weekend camp, and I sat in the backseat wondering how to explain what had just happened to me. I said, "Guess what, Mom and Dad! I know Jesus. I'm going to heaven, and you're not." That wasn't the right thing to say, and it wasn't accurate. I'm still amazed by their relative restraint. It's a little embarrassing to tell that story. Obviously, when I "came out of the world," I leaped wholeheartedly into that smug, self-righteous, Christian subculture that most people don't trust (even when they're in it). But many of us instinctively know something that the adolescent version of me didn't know: the Kingdom of God is a Revolution in regard to the world, but it's also a Revolution in regard to any religious system based on rules, on guilt, on power, on judgment, on shame, on good works—on anything other than love.

Here's the deal. Seventy percent of Americans don't go to church regularly. They—and maybe you—have given up on church. But most haven't given up on God. I know America is supposed to be a "Christian" nation, but most people in America don't know God. They don't understand the uniqueness of Jesus. They have this vague sense that, in the end, all religions are the same. But where are they going to get the truth? *Oprah*? *Good*

Morning America? They might even have a hard time getting the story at a lot of churches. (But 70 percent of Americans aren't there anyway. They don't like church.)

WHEN I WAS THIRTY years old, my wife Libby and our two kids moved to Cincinnati to start a church for people who don't like church. Eleven revolutionary people invited us to leave our lifelong hometown of Pittsburgh, all of our immediate family and friends, and (most wrenchingly) the Pittsburgh Steelers to go after a dream— the dream of helping people like us who hadn't given up on God but had given up on the kind of religion that the typical church practiced.

The church took off from day one. We grew and grew and grew. It wasn't because we were the new, cool church. It was because our church is a place where our friends who have normal questions and objections can challenge and be challenged in an honest and loving way.

We are speaking a language that people who don't know Jesus can understand, even if in the early stages they disagree. People like Rick. He was a smart guy who thought that believing and following Jesus was naïve. With an undergrad degree from Notre Dame and an MBA from Duke, he wasn't going to just check his brain at the door. Years ago he walked up to me after a church service, handed me his business card and boldly said, "I disagree with what you said today." Now he's been able to wrap his brain around the validity of having faith in Jesus. And then there are people like Paula. She was dealing with an addiction, and she found a place where she and her family could come bruised and battered and still be accepted. Then there were the hundreds of people who were just average Joes and Jills who didn't have major problems but did have an inner longing for something more.

As these people came to our church and interacted with people who knew Jesus, they were exposed to things they could never get on CNN or *SportsCenter*. And they started to come alive. It thrills me still that the majority of people who come to Crossroads for a weekend service tell us either that they're not Christ-followers or that they've become Christ-followers since being a part of our community because we don't need another church that only pulls people from other churches. We're after people who might not even like church—people seeking something authentic and bold, people with questions, and people who desire to find something bigger than themselves.

All this sounds like a dream come true. But here's the crazy thing: even this kind of success gets very hollow very fast if you forget that you're part of a Revolution that's a whole lot bigger than you or your petty little empire.

I'll never forget a day soon after we had bought, renovated, and moved into our first building. Our congregation had tripled from 1,500 people showing up on the weekend to 4,500 in less than six months. As I sat by myself on a couch in our 30,000-square-foot atrium, I thought, *So this is it? We just get bigger and bigger and then build a bigger building? Then what? We raise more money and then build again? What's the point?* I had become consumed with the mechanics of building a church—all the things required to maintain a large organization and take care of a huge facility. Without even realizing it, I had again fallen prey to the religious system. And in that moment I was consumed by a longing that was eerily similar to the longing I had before I knew Jesus.

This is what had happened: I had forgotten that the Kingdom of God is about a holistic love for everything God is excited about in this world, not just in small Christian corners. The Kingdom of God goes way beyond church walls and statistics and growth campaigns. We can't run away from the world. We have to run to it.

For the second time in my life, I left religion, and I reenlisted in the Revolution.

THE KINGDOM OF GOD isn't a subculture—a subculture operates apart from what's happening in the larger culture, so the culture doesn't pay it much attention. Neither is the Kingdom of God a counterculture that isolates itself from the mainstream. The Moral Majority of the 1980s was a counterculture. It accomplished little besides angering the mainstream American population and giving Bible-believing Christians a bad name.

David Kinnaman and Gabe Lyons's book *unChristian* lays out the results of a Barna Group survey of younger Americans who were "outsiders" to Christian churches. The researchers wanted to see what people outside the church thought about Christians. Their findings were revealing—and completely depressing:

> In our national surveys with young people, we found the three most common perceptions of present day Christianity are anti-homosexual (an image held by 91 percent of young outsiders), judgmental (87 percent), and hypocritical (85 percent). These "big three" are followed by the following negative perceptions, embraced by a majority of young adults: old-fashioned, too involved in politics, out of touch with reality, insensitive to others, boring, not accepting of other faiths, and confusing.[4]

---

4. David Kinnaman and Gabe Lyons, *unChristian: What a New Generation Really Thinks about Christianity . . . and Why It Matters* (Grand Rapids, MI: Baker, 2007), 27.

That's not what the Kingdom of God is about. The Kingdom of God is not a subculture or a counterculture, but the Kingdom of God does exert a counterforce, and that counterforce is love. The Kingdom of God rebels against the world, but it also rebels against the religious establishment, because in the long run, love shapes people and cultures more effectively than any other force.

Look at the word Revolution. Right in the middle of it, you can see the word love. Maybe it will help if I write it like this: rEVOLution. It's spelled backward. So there, at the center of the Kingdom, is the way of love. And it seems like a backward answer. It always seems backward—the last thing you would have guessed. If you want to find your life, you have to lose it. The first shall be last. The meek shall inherit the earth. If you want to live to the fullest, you have to die to yourself. In sharp contrast, the world operates according to power, prestige, and perks. The world says, "Look out for Number One." The Kingdom says, "Love your neighbor; turn the other cheek; go the extra mile." In other words, the Kingdom of God is a kingdom of love, and it's surprise after surprise. It's unexpected, mysterious, wild, and extravagant. And it's the future—because Jesus won't be finished until He has conquered the whole world.

This good news on a global scale is also good news for you individually. Just as the Kingdom is winning the world, the Revolution will overtake you as well. The Bible is very clear that "he [God] who began a good work in you will be faithful to complete it."[5] At times, you'll be very frustrated by what seems like a lack of progress in areas such as managing your money, controlling your mouth, or stopping your wandering eyes. Or, like me, you might get caught in the rigidity of a religious system and need to fight

---

5. Philippians 1:6, paraphrase

your way back out. But as time goes on, you will look back and notice significant and distinct growth in yourself. You'll see the transformation.

One thing is for sure: the future is golden compared to now. The Bible makes it clear that the world isn't going to hell in a handbasket. The Kingdom of God has always been advancing. It isn't some dead religion. It's vibrant and growing. Jesus is moving forward. His followers are gaining momentum.

So no matter how you've lived or what you've done, Jesus pursues you—and He won't stop. He isn't intimidated or scared away by choices you've made. One of His qualifications to lead the Revolution is that He understands common people, screwed-up people, passionate people with hard questions; He understands all of us. And He comes to you, just as He went to Matthew, saying—simply—"Follow Me." And then freedom is yours.

REVOLUTION

At Crossroads, it's exciting to see ten thousand people show up in our church building each weekend. But what really excites us is the fact that thousands of those people are finding Jesus for the first time, and those people have incredible stories. Throughout the pages of this book, you will read the stories of these real-life revolutionaries as they talk about what God has done in them and through them.

LETTER FROM A REVOLUTIONARY

BEFORE PURSUING A LIFE WITH JESUS, I LED A LIFE THAT WAS TOTALLY ABOUT CONSUMPTION: LIVING IN A NICE HOUSE, DRIVING A NICE CAR, EATING IN THE BEST RESTAURANTS, TAKING THE BEST VACATIONS. MY WHOLE LIFE REVOLVED AROUND THE ASSUMPTION THAT SOMEDAY—WHEN I HAD IT ALL—I'D HAVE A "FULFILLED" LIFE. BUT NOT ONE THING I EVER ACHIEVED, OWNED, ATE, SAW, OR HEARD EVER BROUGHT ME THE NIRVANA I EXPECTED TO GET WHEN I "HAD IT ALL."

NOW I'VE ACCEPTED JESUS INTO MY LIFE, AND I UNDERSTAND GRACE. I UNDERSTAND GOD ANSWERS EVERY PROBLEM IN THE WORLD, AND FOR MANY PEOPLE, I CAN BE A PART OF THAT ANSWER. I NOW KNOW THAT LIFE HAS NOTHING TO DO WITH CONSUMING STUFF BUT ABOUT MAKING A CONTRIBUTION TO THE WORLD.

I NOW HAVE KNOWLEDGE OF HOW SMALL I'VE MADE MYSELF IN THIS WORLD. GOD CREATED ME TO LIVE A LIFE MUCH LARGER THAN I CAN POSSIBLY SEE. OFTEN I'M OVERWHELMED BY THE COMMISSION GOD HAS FOR ME. BUT WHEN I'M QUIET AND ALLOW GOD TO COME INTO MY LIFE, HE INSTILLS IN ME THE COURAGE TO FOCUS NOT ON THE CHALLENGES BUT ON THE DESTINATION.

CH-2

THE REVOLUTION IS ABOUT YOUR FREEDOM

Braveheart is my favorite movie, hands down. It's a movie about one of our deepest human desires: the desire for freedom. And for the sake of freedom, William Wallace and his rowdy, dreadlocked followers go through incredible hardship; they deprive themselves of safety, security, and some pretty basic comforts. They face impossible odds on the battlefield because they'd rather die than live under the thumb of a foreign oppressor. That scene at the end of the movie is unforgettable: even as Wallace's body is being literally torn apart, the cry of his heart—his very last word—is "Freeeeedoooom!"

It's the cry of our hearts, too.

One of the reasons people aren't excited about the idea of God—or at least what has come to be considered the traditional God of the Bible—is that we're afraid He'll stamp out our "freedom." We're afraid He'll make us stop doing the things that give us happiness. We're afraid He'll ask us to wear religious lapel pins, hand out leaflets on the corner, and stop drinking anything stronger than Hawaiian Punch.

Believe it or not, God understands how you feel. He understands your passion for freedom because He's the one who put that intensity and passion in you. He wired you that way. Why? Because that desire for freedom points you back to Him.

It's one of life's biggest ironies: we run from God because we're afraid He's going to take away our freedom, but freedom is exactly what God wants for us. Freedom is what He made us for. And here's the key: He's the only one who can give it.

You've seen people—maybe you are one—who look like they've got all the freedom in the world. I have a good friend named Scott who does exactly as he pleases. He has beautiful women. He has athletic talent. He has money. He has the Porsche *and* the new Land Rover. If he ever told them, I know he'd have story after story of escapades that every red-blooded male in his thirties would love to live. Sometimes I run into him when I'm having breakfast at a diner in town, and it's clear from those bloodshot eyes and tired smile that Scott's been out enjoying his freedom, all wild-night long.

But all that "freedom" has Scott in bondage. He used to have a beautiful wife, but now he's "free" from her because she left him. And now he doesn't have a normal family life with his kids either. Because he's his own boss, there's no steady income, and he's chained to a lifestyle he can't afford. Nothing grounds him, so he floats from moment to moment, and he's running dry. Thankfully, he's looking for new answers. He's beginning to realize that the life he's living has nothing to do with freedom.

It's amazing what people will give up so they can have what they think they want. The truth is that freedom comes when we understand where we're going and when our feet are "planted."

Having a relationship with God isn't about giving up your freedom. It's about getting back the freedom we human beings gave up a long, long time ago. Freedom is where we started. It's what God made us for. And all that energy and effort we spend trying to get our freedom back is literally wasted if we aren't looking to God to do what only He can do.

We're all part of what I call the "Cycle of Freedom." We had it, we lost it, and now we're looking to get it back. The Revolution is about that big wheel making a big revolution so that we're back on top—and free again.

THE CYCLE OF FREEDOM

1) FREEDOM

Genesis is the first book of the Bible. It talks about where we came from and how everything in this world got started. In the very first chapter of the very first book, we see exactly what God designed: an amazing place for humans to live. When God gave the earth to Adam and Eve (the first people he created in the Bible), He implied they could be as imaginative as they wanted. They could build their homes, create businesses, name the plants and animals, have amazing sex, and populate the earth. He didn't micromanage. He didn't make demands or passive-aggressive suggestions. He gave an open canvas and said, "Have at it."

God didn't create bionic, boring, choiceless people. He created men and women He could be in a genuine relationship with. If He had wanted to prescribe all our movements, He would have preloaded us with Microsoft God. But He didn't. He didn't tell Adam and Eve how to spend their time. He gave them rule over all the creatures of the earth, but He didn't tell them *how* to; He trusted them to figure it out. In the same way, God doesn't prescribe what your occupation should be, what car you should buy, or whom you should marry. You have choices.

So from the beginning, we had freedom. The only thing God told Eve and Adam not to do was eat from the Tree of Knowledge of Good and Evil. It wasn't a tree that would provide greater choice or all the answers that are so exciting to know. It was a tree that would expose Adam and Eve to evil, something they hadn't yet known or had to deal with. So God was asking them to trust Him, have faith, and follow something they didn't fully understand. (Sound familiar?)

> **Satan:** a spiritual being who leads a force that is against God and against your freedom and who wants to separate you from Jesus and the life He offers.

I know what you're thinking: Why such an arbitrary rule? Who cares whether or not two people eat the fruit of a particular tree? I don't know that I can give an answer that will satisfy you . . . and I'm okay with that. God is God because He's wiser than we are. But I do know this: Adam and Eve had amazing freedom. They could eat the fruit of every other tree in the whole place. They were in mind-blowing paradise that had only one restriction. Yet Adam and Eve didn't honor the wishes of a freedom-giving God because they thought they could find a better way.

Earlier, I talked about the irony that our desire for freedom—a desire that should point us back to God—often causes us to reject God. That seems about as backward as love being the answer to the Revolution, doesn't it? Well, that irony goes all the way back to the Garden of Eden.

When Satan tempted Eve, telling her God was holding back and didn't have her best interest in mind, he distorted what was actually going on. Satan tried to convince Eve that obeying God would restrict her freedom. He said, "God knows that when you eat of it your eyes will be opened, and you will be like God, knowing good and evil."[1] Do you see what's going on here? God had made Adam and Eve in His own image.[2] He wasn't holding back at all. He gave perfectly—even going so far as to give His creation the choice to choose *against* Him. Sounds like total freedom to me.

Unfortunately, along with the ability to choose comes the ability to choose poorly. Adam and Eve used their freedom to eat the fruit that God said not to eat. They opened themselves up to evil—a burden that God would have carried Himself. A burden God was rescuing us from.

Since God had created a perfect world, it could only get worse. Perfection doesn't evolve. It can only devolve. When we make bad choices, things get worse. You may be very upset by the calamity in our world today—murder, kidnapping, starvation, prejudice, hatred, apathy, thievery, oppression. But God doesn't cause those things. Those things come because God allows people to use (and abuse) their freedom. And everything dark and evil—everything

---

1. Genesis 3:5
2. Genesis 1:26–27

imperfect—was uncorked that day in the garden, and it was uncorked not by God, but by man.

God could have created and maintained a fail-safe world. But you can't have perfection and human freedom at the same time.

2) FALL

The Fall refers to the fact that all of creation fell from a previous state of perfection and completion, and the effects of Adam and Eve's first sin continue all the way up to the present. Though we weren't actually there when Adam and Eve made their bad choice, they were our representatives before God. They opened up the possibility of sin: "Therefore, just as sin entered the world through one man, and death through sin . . . in this way death came to all men, because all [have] sinned." [3]

Sin entered the world through one man and one woman. Maybe it doesn't sound right that each of us should suffer the effects of a bad choice that was made ages ago. "Hmmm," you might say. "I don't remember having a chance to vote for that one. Why should I inherit a world and a life infected by sin?"

Come on now. Do you really think you would have done any

---

3. Romans 5:12

differently? Have you ever been able to go a day without making a sinful, selfish choice? We all inherited that rebellious gene. And that's just part of it. There's also the fact that God created each of us with the freedom to choose—which, as I said earlier, includes the freedom to choose badly.

Every day I am reminded that I am affected and infected by the Fall, whether I'm fighting unfairly with my wife, Libby, or finding pleasure in someone else's failure because it makes me feel better about myself. The other day, for instance, I found myself joking about someone just to get people to laugh. It was a cheap laugh that demeaned another person and revealed how insecure and sometimes sinfully juvenile I can be.

All that is not right about this world can be traced back to the effects of sin. If there were no bad choices, there would be no diseases, no death, and no need for 55 mph speed limits. This world has been poisoned with sin. And that makes it even harder to use our freedom to make good choices.

All of us eventually find ourselves in a free fall away from the kind of life we always wanted. Of course, there are those few who never realize they have a problem. Others don't feel themselves spiraling out of control until they're on their deathbed (and the last time I checked, the death rate was hovering right around 100 percent). Eventually, most of us come to realize that something is wrong and that we need something, anything, to help us.

Sometimes the realization comes with the diagnosis of a terminal disease. Other times it comes when divorce or bankruptcy rocks a person's world. And some people end up "getting it all" but realize something is still missing. They have made more money than they ever thought they would. They have had more and better sex than the average guy, and they've ultimately won the popularity contest. Yet those things don't satisfy. The great French mathematician and philosopher Blaise Pascal dubbed this lack of satisfaction our "God-shaped vacuum." And you can guess who needs to fill it.

3) FAITH

Sooner or later, all of us put our faith somewhere. Maybe you've put your faith in your kindness to strangers or your diligent work. Or maybe you're one of those sadists who think the answer lies in trying even harder to please God, so you've put your faith in your own efforts. You keep thinking that the intended results are just around the corner. You think, *I'll give more money. I'll help more poor people. I'll pray longer. I'll go to church more often. I'll vote straight Republican. I'll vote straight Democrat. I won't smoke. I won't chew. I won't date the girls who do.*

The problem is, those solutions won't ultimately satisfy your spirit. They never will. You keep hoping that something will click and you'll get some fulfillment from those things, but they haven't done anything for you—or they haven't done enough, anyway. If they had, you probably wouldn't still be reading this book.

Some of us put faith in the latest self-help system or the newest leadership guru's method for self-improvement. These things aren't inherently bad or sinful; it's just that they're insufficient because they still place the responsibility for true change on you. And let's be honest: you just don't have it in you. Sooner or later, you'll realize this, if you haven't already.

So you have to ask yourself what you've put your faith in. Can I tell you something not to put your faith in? Religion.

Religion is not the same as faith. Religion is a set of principles and practices that may help us connect with God, but religion is not God. No person, no organization, no tradition, no liturgy is God. As committed as I am to the church I pastor, as much as I love it, my church is not God. Only God is God.

Please understand me. I'm not trying to pick a fight with any specific religion or any particular spiritual practice. If you want to go up on a mountain with crystals and chant, that's your business. Have fun. If you want to mindlessly sit through a religious service on Sunday morning because you think it will get you on God's good side, be my guest. Play church. But I've found that if things like this aren't silly, they are at least forms of bondage because they keep you locked into a system that isn't bringing lasting freedom.

> **Religion:** any system of practices that is worked in order to earn God's approval.

Take Hinduism, for example. You think reincarnation and karma sound like good things? What about the fact that Hinduism says that everything bad in your life is your fault? And if you want to come back as something cool—if you really don't want to be turned into a poodle—you better have a plan for being the wisest, most sincere, most loving person ever. The way I see it, that's not freedom. That's bondage. That's an anxiety-driven, smothering-under-guilt way of life. Everything depends on you, and you can only get according to what you can do.

So if you're putting your faith in something that relies on your own power because God doesn't do anything for you, think about what that actually means. Sooner or later, something will come along that you can't handle, and your power just won't be enough.

I'm not walling myself up in my own little church here or avoiding what others consider truth. I'm evaluating and putting other beliefs to the test. It's not my goal to put down every other religion. After all, many folks in religious systems are doing amazing things. However, it is my goal to look for the God who really is and then decide about the veracity or credibility of the belief in question. And I encourage you to do the same. Whatever your spirituality is, ask yourself a few questions:

- Do I feel close to a specific God, or is mine a general spirituality?
- Do I have a deep inner satisfaction that isn't fading?
- Am I praying for things and actually seeing answers or feeling a response?
- Do I know people who have followed this path for twenty to thirty years? Do they have the kind of life I aspire to have?

One guy who evaluated his religion was Paul. He was a hard-core, all-star Jew. He had memorized all the Jewish Scriptures (also known as the Old Testament). He did everything necessary to be kosher: he followed every rule and probably made a lot of sacrifices. He came to realize, however, that all he had attained didn't really matter. It didn't bring him a meaningful and personal connection with God. It didn't give him a powerful prayer life.

WELCOME TO THE REVOLUTION

Something was missing. That something was a relationship with God's Son, Jesus. Here's how Paul explained a key insight from his personal journey:

> I consider everything a loss compared to the surpassing greatness of knowing Christ Jesus my Lord, for whose sake I have lost all things. I consider them rubbish, that I may gain Christ and be found in him, not having a righteousness of my own that comes from the law, but that which is through faith in Christ—the righteousness that comes from God and is by faith.[4]

Paul realized that he was on a spiritual treadmill. Religious exercises kept him busy, but they didn't get him anywhere. He had faith, and plenty of it, but it wasn't faith in what ultimately works: Jesus. When Paul came into a relationship with Jesus, he found what he needed to stop his spiritual insanity. He got off the spiritual, religion-propelled treadmill and found a loving, generous God. He found freedom.

Hopefully, you're exercising your mind as well as your freedom to choose and asking yourself, *Who is Brian Tome, or who is Paul, to say that they have found the real answer? How do I know that Jesus really is the way? How do I know they haven't just found something that works for them but wouldn't work for me?* If you aren't asking these kinds of questions, you should be.

And here's how I would answer them: I've chosen to place my faith in Jesus. My faith in Him is real. My faith in Him is concrete, because He is concrete. He has a personality and an existence. I'm not making things up or creating a cut-and-paste kind of God. I'm not just saying, "This works for me." I'm saying, "It works—

---

4. Philippians 3:8–9

period." The truths of the Gospel have stood the test of time because Jesus is God. Millions have followed Jesus—thousands who met Him, saw Him killed, and then saw Him come back to life. And millions upon millions are still following Him.

And while we're at it, millions upon millions believed in Jesus before He actually came to Earth. Hundreds of years before Jesus was

> **Prophets:** spiritual leaders in the Bible whom God spoke through in order to get a message to His people.

born, prophets like Isaiah and Jeremiah were talking about the coming Messiah.

Their prophecies detailed everything: where He would be born, the virgin who would give birth to Him, where He would minister, and even how He would die. They predicted that this Messiah, God's Son, would be betrayed by a kiss from a friend and nailed to a tree. One prophecy even mentioned that a spear would be stuck in His side, yet not a single bone would be broken. Another said that people would gamble for His clothes after His death, only to see Him in fresh clothes after He came back from the dead three days later.

Do you realize that every single one of those prophecies was fulfilled? Every single one! And there are other prophecies. None of these foretold events happened by chance. God was getting the world ready for the Messiah, His Son, our Hero, to provide a way out of the condition that sin had put us in.

Jesus' death on the cross is how God chose to deal with and resolve our sinfulness. God doesn't run away from things. He doesn't leave us fallen and hopeless. He chose to deal with our sin by sending the only Person who could pay the debt we incurred by our first rebellion—and continual rebellion—against God. Only Jesus could satisfy God's justice. Only Jesus could be the ultimate showing of God's love.

People who are offended by the bloodiness of the cross don't understand how sinful we are and how just and full of grace God is. The cross is a straightforward answer to a straightforward problem. You and I sinned. God was angry (but full of love for us), and so He needed to enact justice. That's what Jesus came to do. That's what Jesus did. He paid the debt that we could not pay ourselves. And in order to be released from our slavery—in order to live the life of freedom that only God can give—you and I need to have faith in Jesus. That's it. That's the simple answer.

Simple, but not easy. In order for you to receive the righteousness and forgiveness of Jesus and receive a faith that really matters—a faith that will really change your life and all that lies ahead—you have to surrender every bit of yourself to God. You might think to yourself, *Why would I do that?* You would do it because you sense the Revolution happening inside your heart.

Forgiveness: releasing any claim that you have on another person—even a rightful claim—that the world tells you to nurture and hold on to. These claims include bitterness, the desire for revenge, and financial debts. The Kingdom tells us to let go—to release and kill what is spiritually and emotionally killing us.

You would do it because you long for freedom that you can't get any other way. You would do it because it's a good trade—your hurt for God's healing; your emptiness for God's abundance; your crap for God's riches.

Forgiveness always costs somebody something.

Years ago, a friend of mine dropped me off at the airport in my Jeep. Instead of going back home, he went four-wheeling, crushed the fender, broke off the antenna, and basically submerged it in mud. Well, he didn't have the money to fix it. I chose to forgive the debt. (And that was hard. It was a pretty cool Jeep.) It wasn't that the damage went away. Someone still had to pay for it; it just wasn't my friend. I paid for it. Forgiving my friend cost me. Our forgiveness cost God. It cost God His Son.

Earlier in this chapter we talked about the possibility that it wasn't fair that Adam and Eve's sin caused trouble for the rest of us. The truth is, we don't need fairness. We need grace. We need God to do for us what we cannot do for ourselves. We need God to give us what we don't deserve. And it is grace, not fairness, that compels God to pay our debt. And that is love.

You don't have to be comfortable with the idea that one man's sin wrecked things for the rest of history. But I hope you will celebrate the truth that one Man's obedience made a way for the damage to be repaired. The Bible tells us, "For just as through the disobedience of the one man the many were made sinners, so also through the obedience of the one man the many will be made righteous."[5]

Just as Adam and Eve's poor choice led to our sin and downward spiral, so also Jesus' good choice to die a death He didn't deserve can lead to our righteousness in God's eyes.

---

5. Romans 5:19

If your faith isn't in Christ, you're on a treadmill that will never get you anywhere. You'll stay in the same place running and running, spiritualizing and spiritualizing, theorizing and theorizing, even praying and praying. But the awesome thing about God's Kingdom is that you can get off the treadmill. You can break out of selfishness and loneliness and addiction and get into a purposeful life.

When you come to true faith in Jesus Christ, you get real power. You get the Holy Spirit, and He enables you to have "works" that are worth something—worth something to your personal growth, worth something to God, worth something to the advancing Kingdom. And this is what is called genuine fruit.

4) FRUITS

God wants us to work hard and have an abundant life characterized by good deeds. But good deeds aren't the way we get to God. Good deeds happen naturally after we have faith in Jesus and understand what to do with it. We don't earn a relationship with God through hard work, no matter what this individualistic society tells us. Instead, we enjoy a relationship with Jesus that drives us to do things that matter. In fact, if you aren't seeing any tangible change in your life, then you have to question whether or not you really are in a relationship with God.

"I am the vine; you are the branches. If a man remains in me and I in him, he will bear much fruit; apart from me you can do nothing."[6]

You can obviously do a lot of nice and compassionate things without being a Christ-follower. But none of those things mean anything to God if they aren't springing from a relationship with Him. In a relationship with Him, we will be able to do great things (bear genuine fruit) that bring pleasure both to God and to us. This is the freedom—what the Bible also calls the "times of refreshing"—that comes from God.[7]

FREE AGAIN

God doesn't want you to try harder. He wants you to give up. He wants you to surrender. He wants you to turn to him and accept the freedom and adventure He offers.

Now the Lord is the Spirit, and where the Spirit of the Lord is, there is freedom.[8]

It is for freedom that Christ has set us free.[9]

All God wants for you is to be free. And even though you screw things up and make awful and destructive choices, God says that He will forgive you if you are in a love relationship with Him. You just have to ask.

---

6. John 15:5
7. Acts 3:19
8. 2 Corinthians 3:17
9. Galatians 5:1

If you're ready to ask—if you're ready to put your faith in Christ—just communicate that to God and give up all your previous notions and counterfeit systems for attaining a fulfilled life. And what you say to Him isn't so much about the words as it is the intent. It can be this simple: "God, I realize that my way hasn't worked. I want to try Your way by surrendering control of my life to You and Your Son, Jesus. Please come into my life and allow me to serve You. Thank You for this chance."

If you've decided to follow Jesus, you've gotten back on top of the Cycle of Freedom. You're back where God wanted you all along. Back to freedom and released from the bondage of sin and the burden of trying harder. Like William Wallace in *Braveheart*, you've painted your face blue, jumped on a horse, and are riding out to battle. Because you know what you need. You know what to fight for . . . freedom!

FREEDOM:
LETTER FROM A REVOLUTIONARY

My life was a repetition of sporadic and impulsive decision making and action taking with zero accountability. I was self-centered, defensive, careless, aggressive, and unforgiving. Don't get me wrong. I have good qualities too, but I always chose to skim over the rough edges of my character and not be accountable to God. I thought that a life of action meant living deliberately, but without a true north to give guidance, all that happens is you keep ending up in the same place . . . just different scenery.

I no longer wish to be hopeless, always expecting the worst things to happen. Life without Jesus is hopeless, so I choose God. The last year and a half, my spirituality has slowly been growing, but I have been reluctant to share this with my family, friends, co-workers, and boyfriend. I didn't want to be perceived as a stereotypical crazy Christian woman that people avoided. My pride and insecurities were more important than my relationship with God.

But in the last three months, the awakening of my spirituality has made me realize that the path I had chosen for my life was the one God wanted for me. I'd been extremely independent and kept my loved ones a great distance away from the authentic me. I left my family and the man I loved dearly, all to obtain what I wanted for myself. Then it occurred to me that the closer I was to obtaining my idea of success, the more restless I was becoming.

God was missing in my life on a daily basis. I realized that moving away from home and chasing my idea of success was not God's definition of success for me. Living a life alone and unattached to a community is not God's way. Living life with God means having an intimate relationship with Him, thereby creating and participating in a community blessed by God.

God is my salvation from myself and from the world. My life is changing completely. I am leaving my job and moving back home to be with family and friends, and to continue my journey with God at a church community that I can connect with and grow through.

A NEW MOVEMENT

So if the Revolution is moving forward, how do you as an individual take part in it? What's your role? That's what the rest of this book is about—the disciplines of spiritual formation that will equip and empower you to play your part in the Revolution of the Kingdom of God.

This is the part of the book where you might expect me to say something like this: *If the Revolution is going to move forward, it depends on the disciplined efforts of foot soldiers like you.* That's not what I'm going to say. Instead, I'm going to say this: *The Revolution is going forward with or without you. But the Revolution of the Kingdom of God is something you don't want to miss.* And since God is always at work, spiritual formation is simply a matter of jumping in and then staying in the flow of what God is doing in the world and in your life. You can do that in many ways, but the most important are prayer, Bible reading, community, and mission.

Prayer. Bible reading. Community. Mission. That doesn't sound all that revolutionary, does it? But what is revolutionary is realizing that these things aren't a way to build your spiritual resume or chalk up brownie points with God. They aren't even the basic training activities that will enable you to go out and kick butt on God's behalf. Prayer, Bible reading, community, and mission are simply the way you stay in the flow of what God is doing. Understand that, practice that, and you'll find yourself involved in some incredible, revolutionary things.

When I talk about "staying in the flow," that's not the same thing as "going with the flow." I'm not talking about being passive or taking the path of least resistance. The things of the world flow in a different direction from the things of God. We've all been affected by the Fall, so when we live to please ourselves or to please others, we inevitably end up drifting away from God, and we get out of sync with what He's doing. It takes discipline to stay in the flow of the Revolution. It takes a daily choice.

Back when I first started following Jesus, I realized that underage drinking was going to pull me out of God's flow for my life. I knew I couldn't go with the flow of my friends, but I had to figure out what that would look like. Well, it looked like apple juice in a plastic beer cup. Before you assume I was going into hiding about my faith, think about it this way: when we follow Jesus, we don't suddenly detach ourselves from the world. We don't curl up in a Christian corner and die off. If it's not unhealthy, we stay with people who don't yet know Jesus, and we don't judge them or scare them off with a huge bumper sticker that says, "I'm going to heaven—and you're NOT."

It's the same idea as waiting until after I've built relationships with the guys on the basketball court before telling them that I'm a pastor. The relationship building comes first. So when I stopped getting plastered, I went against the previous flow of my life—the flow that my friends were still in—and got in the flow of where God was taking me.

NEW CONSTRUCTION

There will be some big changes as you enter into your new life with Jesus. It has been said that "The only people who like being changed are babies with dirty diapers."[1] Maybe that's why Jesus said, "Unless you become like a child, you will never enter the kingdom of heaven."[2] Being like a child means maintaining a teachable heart and wanting to change. Think about it: both physically and mentally, children grow faster than anybody. They can assimilate a new skill or a new language faster and more easily than an adolescent or an adult. That's probably because they're more pliable and less rooted in their ways. And that's one of the most exciting things about being a new follower of Jesus. You aren't as set in your spiritual ways as a person who has spent a lifetime toeing the religious line.

When I was younger, I spent several summers doing construction work. Some of it was new construction, and some was remodeling. My boss classified all jobs as either "grunt work" or "glory work." With new construction, there was a little grunt work—like digging ditches, wheeling wheelbarrows, filling dumpsters—but mostly it was glory work. And that was the fun stuff, the work that gave you a sense of accomplishment. You frame a wall, you raise the wall, and soon you have a structure where there wasn't anything before. Glory work.

Remodeling isn't nearly so glorious. You may build a wall, but first you've got to tear out the old wall. And while you're tearing out the old wall, you've got to pull out the old wiring—and watch out for that existing plumbing! You don't want to puncture

---

1. From book *Beyond a Government of Strangers* by Robert Maranto, p. 7
2. Matthew 18:3, paraphrase

a copper line. And then there's the roofing. Roofing's bad enough under the best of circumstances, but on a remodel you've got to rip off the old shingles first, which might reveal rotten wood that has to be replaced. I once fell through a rotting roof and straight into an attic (a moment when I really missed the glory work of new construction).

If you're a new Christ-follower with zero religious experience, spiritual training, or previous convictions, what's going on in your life is probably a mixture of new construction and remodeling. Both the glory and the grunt. Many people who have been in churches or have been professing Christians for decades just desperately need to remodel. There are layers of sin or bad information that need to be ripped off. Rather than dealing with problems, they have wallpapered over rotten wood and neglected the foundational elements of their spiritual houses. There is hope for them, of course. No spiritual house is beyond repair. But they can't just build from where they are. They must first go back and tear down poor habits and wrong assumptions before they can add on.

You undoubtedly have bad habits and bad assumptions as well. You probably had some sort of spirituality that was ill formed. But at least your bad habits and bad assumptions weren't accumulated under the auspices of "Christianity." At least you don't have any illusions that the God of the Bible validated those things. That's one advantage you have over people who have been professing Christians for a long time.

But you need to know that there is no special spiritual insight that will instantly make you like Jesus. There are no shortcuts, no "Three Easy Steps to Spiritual Maturity." Growth is gradual. Sure, there will be occasional turbo boosts. You may find yourself in a worship service and something will be said from the front that rocks your world. Or you'll be talking to a friend, and some-thing he or she says just hits you as spiritual truth. Or you'll be creating art, and suddenly something happens inside of you that you didn't expect, and it will no longer be a time of creating art but a sacred moment between you and God that you can't really explain. Those are moments of extra grace, and they definitely help you get more into the flow of what God is doing.

But no matter how many turbo boosts you have—and we all wish we could have more—it takes time and patience to become the person God wants you to be. Our time on Earth is filled with the hard work of eliminat-ing sin from our lives and adding in other things that are pleasing to God, all the while ad-vancing His Kingdom and blessing others. I'm not saying that it's up to you to eliminate the bad and add the good by using all your own strength. I'm saying that it's up to you to stay in the flow, day by day, and put yourself in a position where God will do His work in you. As one Christ-follower in the Bible said, "He who began a good work in you will carry it on to completion until the day of Christ Jesus."[3]

> **Grace:** a blessing God gives us, even though we've done nothing to deserve it, and any punishment God with-holds even though we do deserve it.

I'm walking a tightrope here. It is God who does the real work of making us into the people He wants us to be. We can't forget that. But we have a part to play too—and we'd better not forget that.

---

3. Philippians 1:6

SPIRITUAL DISCIPLINES

I've always wanted to run a marathon. At least, that's what I think until I actually run. I'm not a runner. I think it's boring, and I'd rather ride my motorcycle. Still, though, I've entertained the idea and even had long talks with a marathoner who says he'll give me an awesome training plan to get me through the day-to-day. Following Jesus is much the same way. You don't finish or win a marathon—you don't stay in God's flow—just by trying your best and using all your natural faculties. You train. You train intentionally.

Here's what one of Jesus' followers, Paul, had to say on the subject:

> Everyone who competes in the Olympics goes into strict training. They do it to get recognition that will not last; but the Christ follower does it to get recognition that will last forever.[4]

We understand discipline when it comes to training for the Olympics. We understand discipline when it comes to being an honor student. And we understand discipline when it comes to advancing our careers. In all of these realms, success requires that we intentionally structure key components or disciplines into our lives and follow through repeatedly until what we've envisioned actually takes shape.

That's what spiritual formation is: envisioning a life wholeheartedly devoted to God and then moving that from vision to reality. We all need to structure the four key components (prayer, Bible reading, community, and mission) into our lives in order to

---

4. 1 Corinthians 9:25, paraphrase

grow in our faith and experience God for all He is worth. In the next chapters, I'll explain what each of these means.

But first let me be clear: God's growth strategy for us includes many other things, including generous financial giving; spending time with those less fortunate than we are; spending time in solitude; and expanding the mind God gave us by reading good books. However, the four key components are the foundation for all the other disciplines.

Picture a three-legged stool. If you've only got one leg, you don't have a stool. But some people try to exist on one leg. Many try to be Christ-followers on the Bible alone. What happens when you take one leg and try to sit on it? Go ahead. Find a wooden dowel or a broom handle and sit on it. That's right. You look like a Bible-only person with a stick up your butt. Do you know any of these people? They're the ones who've kept you from the Revolution instead of wooing you to the Kingdom. You do need the Bible, but you need the other legs as well.

Some people will try to do only community and prayer without a lot of Bible. They're more relationally engaged and lovey-dovey. But eventually their lives tip over. There must be a standard that governs how we relate to others and how we pray. If you don't have the Bible, you cannot stand firm.

But three legs aren't a stool unless they are attached to a seat. The seat is mission. It's what holds everything together and serves as the platform of your life. The goal of the stool isn't the legs; it's the seat. In the same way, the goal of your life isn't to read the Bible, have spiritual community, or even pray to God. The goal of your life involves the Revolution happening in you and your role in bringing the Kingdom to fruition. A lot of different things can rest on top of the stool. The Kingdom, after all, is wide and varied in its activities and goals. Your micro mission may be very different from those of other Christ-followers you know, but you are all part of the macro mission of the same Revolution. The Revolution is that big. The Revolution is that all-encompassing.

If you're looking for a set of rules to follow so you can be a "good Christian," there isn't one. But I can tell you how Jesus summed up a life that pleases God: "Love the Lord your God with all your heart and with all your soul and with all your mind and with all your strength."[5] I know, that might be more intimidating than a set of rules. A set of rules, even if it's hard, is at least something you can be in control of. But Jesus doesn't give you that option. He won't let you control your destiny. You have to surrender.

But as you surrender more and more territory to Jesus—as the Revolution really infiltrates your life—you will find that you're doing your work the way Jesus would work, socializing the way Jesus would socialize, structuring your family the way Jesus would structure a family. You don't do these things to get God's approval. Rather, as a result of God's approval—as Jesus takes up more territory in your life—you desire to stay in the flow. The rest of this book talks about how to do exactly that.

---

5. Mark 12:30

MOVEMENT:
LETTER FROM A REVOLUTIONARY

Growing up, I was concerned about only one thing: getting out of college so I didn't have to return to the coal mines or steel mills of southeastern Ohio. But really, I just wanted to run away from my childhood and family issues. I was concerned with me and only me. I was trampling every relationship: God, friends, family, girlfriends, all of them.

I went from one job to the next. Whichever gave me more money, I was there. So I took a job overseas. I didn't speak the language, and I didn't laugh for six months. I had no relationships with people I cared about or who cared for me. Well, the company I was working for lost half a billion dollars overnight. To make the story shorter, I looked up one night to heaven and confessed to God that I was chasing the wrong things. I asked for His help to get back home, and a month later, I was.

I was financially, spiritually, emotionally, and professionally in need of help. Basically, I had nothing. However, in order for us to grow, God has us experience the death of the bad in us so that we can then accept the good He has planned for us.

I found a healthy church a few months later. I began going on a regular basis and became a part of that community. I was applying what I was learning to my everyday life on an ongoing basis. This was something I'd never experienced before.

Being a part of this church week by week and year by year has helped me reach a point in my life where I have found the strength to reach out for help. I continue to be a healthier person. I could not have done this if I hadn't first asked for Jesus to come into my life.

THE BIBLE

Somebody once asked the famous writer and thinker G. K. Chesterton, "If you were stranded on a desert island and could only have one book, which book would it be?" Chesterton was an eloquent, outspoken, and influential Christ-follower, so I suspect the person asking the question thought he knew what the answer would be.

But Chesterton wasn't one to follow the script. He didn't answer, "The Bible." If he were stranded on a desert island, the one book Chesterton wanted with him was a practical guide to shipbuilding. After all, that would be the one book that could get him where he wanted to be: home.

Plenty of people treat the Bible as if it were simply an easy and pious answer. "What's the most influential book you've ever read?" "Why, the Bible, of course." See how easy that was? But if the Bible is really going to make a difference in your life, you're going to have to approach it in ways that you may not expect.

The Bible is the one book that can get you where you want to be (that is, if you want to be in the thick of the Kingdom)—but only if you read it. The Bible won't do you any good if you treat it as if it were an icon or an object of worship to be handled carefully and with quiet reverence. If the Bible is going to do its work in you, you've got to be ready to get down and wrestle with it.

Let me put it this way: if the Bible doesn't make you mad every now and then, you probably aren't paying attention. God didn't give you the Bible to make you feel better about yourself. He gave you the Bible to change you into the person He wants you to be.

THE BIBLE IS FOR TRANSFORMATION, NOT JUST INFORMATION

The Bible is a personal letter from God to you. He doesn't just want to fill your head with information. He wants to take your heart and make you more like Christ.

You may have heard the Bible described as "the inspired Word of God." I'm trying to stay away from that kind of churchy language in this book, but I do want to explain this one, because it makes a big difference in understanding how the Bible transforms you. The word *inspired* literally means "God-breathed." God breathed His Spirit into the people who physically wrote the Bible.

That's significant for a lot of reasons. For one thing, it means that the Bible is truly God's message, even though human beings—with personalities and cultural contexts—physically wrote it down.

Holy Spirit: the Person of God who inspires, inhabits, and empowers His people.

But here's what I'm really getting at: when the Revolution started in you, God breathed His Spirit into you. The Holy Spirit who is now at work in your life—teaching you, nudging you in this direction or that, telling you when you're not advancing the Kingdom—is the same Spirit who inspired the Bible. That's huge when you think about it. Here's what the Bible says about itself:

> All Scripture is God-breathed and is useful for teaching, rebuking, correcting and training in righteousness, so that the man of God may be thoroughly equipped for every good work.[1]

So this Scripture says God has breathed His word (or truth) into the Bible so that:

1. You can be proactively shown what you need to know (teaching).
2. You can be called on the carpet when you've done wrong (rebuking).
3. You can be pointed in the right direction after being called out (correcting).
4. You can be prepared to do the right thing (training in righteousness).

When all this is happening, you are being thoroughly equipped to do every good work that God wants you to do. This is transformation. God isn't interested in you sitting back and becoming a Bible egghead. He wants the information that is contained in His love letter to you to transform your life and, in turn, to transform everything you touch.

---

1. 2 Timothy 3:16–17

When we describe a book as "inspiring" or "inspirational," we usually mean that the book motivates us to be better people, or maybe it helps us to see the good in others. Nothing is wrong with that. But we mean something different when we say the Bible is "inspired." Hopefully the Bible motivates you to be a better person, but the real point of saying it is "inspired" is that the Holy Spirit is at work in the Bible and in your life at the same time. If the Holy Spirit is working in your life, something happens when you read the Bible that doesn't happen when you read any other book. And if the Holy Spirit isn't at work, the words on the pages of the Bible can't really do their work on you.

One of my favorite movies, next to *Braveheart*, is *What About Bob?* Bill Murray plays the main character, Bob, a hypochondriac, germophobic, deeply neurotic bundle of anxiety. In his first appointment with psychiatrist Dr. Marvin, Bob tries to explain why his marriage broke up. "The world is divided into two types of people," says Bob. "Those who like Neil Diamond and those who don't. My ex-wife loves him."

From behind his mahogany desk, Dr. Marvin gives Bob a little glimpse of reality, the first glimpse he's had in some time:

So, what you're saying is that even though you are an almost-paralyzed, multiphobic personality who's in a constant state of panic, your wife did not leave you; you left her because she liked Neil Diamond?

Bob's face goes blank. He pauses, thinks, and stammers out: "Now y-y-y-you're telling me that maybe I didn't leave my wife because she likes Neil Diamond . . . but that *she* left *me*?"

The doctor nods. Bob pauses again, then clutches his chest and bellows, "Oww! Oww!"

Many times when I read the Bible, my spirit bellows from inside my chest, "Oww! Oww!" These are times when I'm taught, rebuked, corrected, or trained. My messed-up worldview—just as crazy as Bob's—gets exposed by the light of God's truth. And, to be honest, it hurts.

I remember when I was reading the Bible, the book of 2 Kings, about the Israelites building "high places" where they worshipped false gods. God had blessed them incredibly, giving them this beautiful land to live in and driving out the enemies who had occupied it. But as soon as the land was theirs, the Israelites turned from God and started behaving exactly like their enemies had.

Reading about the Israelites made me start thinking about my own life. I, too, had been incredibly blessed—but was I being faithful to the God who had been so faithful to me? I wrote in my prayer journal that day, "Lord, are there 'high places' in my life that I'm protecting from You?"

You'd better be careful what you pray for. If you ask for insight into your own secrets, God is going to give it to you. It wasn't long before God's voice came crashing through in the form of a vivid memory. "Do you remember those pictures you stole two days ago?"

Oww! Oww!

I like to think of myself as an upstanding citizen. I'm a preacher, for crying out loud. But sometimes being an upstanding citizen just means you've gotten good at hiding the worst parts of yourself—or, even worse, justifying the worst parts of yourself.

I had been on vacation with my family in Florida. Roaming photographers were taking pictures of families swimming with dolphins. Up at the cabana you could look at the photos electronically and select the ones you wanted to buy. At fifteen dollars a pop for a 5 x 7, I wasn't looking to buy many. After making our selections, we walked to the other side of the complex to pick up our photos. It was a little chaotic; the harder the people behind the desk worked, the further behind they got. I congratulated myself on my patience. After all, I'm an upstanding citizen. A preacher.

When the woman behind the counter finally served up my pictures, she opened up the envelope and waited for me to smile. Instead, I shook my head. Those weren't the ones I had ordered. One picture was of my wife, Libby; the other, a woman I'd never seen before. But there were no pictures of the kids, and Libby and I agreed ahead of time to only buy shots of the kids. I kept my cool. I'm patient. I'm upstanding.

The employee brought up all the photos on-screen, and we went through them one by one. She disappeared into the back. She came back to the counter to double-check the screen, then returned to the back for what seemed a little longer than necessary. But I'm patient . . . upstanding . . .

When the woman came back to the counter, she triumphantly handed me a new pair of photographs. Or so she thought. "These are the same exact photos," I said. There was a testy tone to my voice. Even upstanding citizens have limits to their patience. "That's my wife, but I didn't order that photo. As for the other girl . . . the naked one . . . no, I've never met her." (I'm kidding about the naked part.)

She went in the back again, and I waited for another five minutes or so. When the woman came back out, she had the right photos, and I was ready to go on my way. But before I left, I thought I would test their customer service. I pointed to the photos beside the cash register and said, "What do you say you let me have that picture of my wife since I had to stand and wait all this time?" She said she couldn't; it was against policy. I was bummed that she didn't seize the opportunity to delight a customer, but I told her, "I understand," and away I went.

About an hour later I had to go back to the same location to pick up something on our way out of the park. As I turned to leave, I noticed all the discarded photos in the same place by the cash register. I looked around and, seeing that everyone was either busy or in the back, I took the picture of Libby and put it in my bag. Out I walked, thinking to myself, *It was going to get thrown away anyway, and I wasn't going to buy it.*

So there I sat two days later, asking God, "Are there any high places in my life?"

I knew exactly what I had done wrong. My high places were the feeling of superiority that kicked in when I wasn't being properly served and my ability to rationalize stealing. I had taken something that wasn't mine. I had been dishonest. I had been deceitful. This realization required action. In fact, not to take action would have been to deceive myself. As the apostle James wrote:

> Do not merely listen to the word, and so deceive yourselves. Do what it says. Anyone who listens to the word but does not do what it says is like a man who looks at his face in a mirror and, after looking at himself, goes away and immediately forgets what he looks like. But the man who looks intently into the perfect law that gives freedom, and continues to do this, not forgetting what he has heard, but doing it—he will be blessed in what he does.[2]

As I've already said, the Spirit who inspired the Bible in the first place is living in you, shaping you. To read the Bible and not put its truths into practice is to resist the work that the Spirit is doing. You might as well look in the mirror with no intention of combing your hair.

---

2. James 1:22–25

The Bible, however, doesn't bind us. It convicts us, but it doesn't restrict us. The real restriction in our lives comes when we don't live the way God wants us to live. That's when our lives break down.

I never used to read instruction manuals, but now I never try to assemble anything of any size without reading how to put it together. Somewhere along the way I realized that manufacturers weren't trying to torture me and take away my fun. Instead, they wanted to serve me by helping me put together something that would actually work. If you try to put your life together without reading and following God's instruction manual, it is just not going to work. And you'll miss the blessing that comes with enjoying a great relationship with your heavenly Father.

I know I keep saying this, but I want to make sure you understand something that a lot of professing Christians don't get: doing the "right" things is a result of your relationship with Jesus, not the means by which you gain His favor. When I urge you to read the Bible, it's not so that you can tend to your checklist. It's because the Bible is an important means by which God communicates with us. And communication is key to a loving relationship. Jesus said,

> If you love me, you will obey what I command. And I will ask
> the Father, and he will give you another Counselor to be with
> you forever—the Spirit of truth . . . he lives with you and will
> be in you.[3]

There are a couple of things going on in those verses. First, we see that obedience is the natural outflow of love. When we love God, we do what He wants us to do. And second, we see that God gives us the Holy Spirit to help us along in our pursuit of

---

3. John 14:15–17

obedience. The Spirit who lives within us counsels us in doing what God wants. God gives us a love letter, and He also gives us an internal personal interpreter. Starsky had Hutch; Randy's got Paula and Simon; Christ-followers have the Holy Spirit.

When I was a new Christ-follower, someone gave me an illustration of how this works: when we are headed toward danger and disobedience, God gives us a flag. The flag pops up and says something like, "If you steal that photo, you will be disobeying me." Too often we just plow right past the warning flag.

I certainly plowed right past when I stole the photo. But a couple of days later, God used the Bible and the Holy Spirit to make me aware of my sin. God chose a time when I was more yielding, not so huffy and self-absorbed and self-justifying. Another flag went up in my mind as I sat there journaling. I've ignored God enough to know that if I plow past that flag again, I will set a precedent. The next time I'll blow by it again. Then it will happen again. Eventually there will be nothing left of the flag except a few threads dangling from a stick. The flag won't function properly, and those threads won't get my attention.

In the moment, I may think I'm getting away with something. In reality, I am losing the ability to hear from God. When I ignore those flags or promptings, I'm telling the Spirit, "Don't talk to me." Eventually, He'll give me my false freedom and say, "Fine." Then who's the loser? Me. When we blow through the flags, we damage God's communication system.

Many people who are where you are in your spiritual formation don't heed this lesson. They live their lives as they always have, keeping themselves in the captain's chair. They go wherever they want and rationalize after the fact.

I-95 is a very heavily traveled highway right outside Greenwich, Connecticut. In the late '80s, a bridge on that interstate just buckled and collapsed. A motorist driving along the highway saw the car in front of him disappear over the edge and plunge into the river below. He pulled over, realizing that if he didn't do something fast, other drivers would suffer the same fate. He got out of his car, stepped into the middle of the road, and started waving wildly at two young guys in an oncoming car. Instead of stopping, the driver blew his horn and swerved around the man who was trying to warn him. The passenger whipped our hero the finger, and the two young men drove right off the bridge to their deaths.

It doesn't pay to ignore signs. When you live your life at seventy miles per hour and blow past flag after flag, you will spiritually shrivel. I've seen it happen to too many people.

I wrote a check and sent it to the resort to pay for the picture I'd stolen.

THE BASICS

Maybe we should slow down. I've been talking about obedience and the Holy Spirit and sin and conviction, and you're probably wondering, *What kind of Bible should I be reading?* or *Where do I start?* or *Do I have to read Deuteronomy since it sounds really weird and I can't even pronounce it?* Okay. Here are some thoughts:

First, if you don't have a Bible beside you right now, please stop reading and go get it. If you don't own a Bible, please stop reading and go buy one. Not much point reading a chapter about reading the Bible if you don't have a Bible to read.

If you are heading out to a Christian bookstore, I should probably give you a little word of warning: there's a lot of stuff there that you don't need—racks and racks of cheesy Christian trinkets that take up valuable retail space. Please resist the urge to buy things to stick on your bumper, paste on your notebooks, hang on your walls, or arrange on your souvenir shelves. Not only is some of that stuff out of line with things you'll find in God's Book, but it's simply bad art. To everyone around you who doesn't know Jesus, that schlock communicates, "Hello, I'm losing touch with reality." Remember, God hasn't called you to be a part of some sort of spiritual club that identifies itself through various displays of religiosity. He has called you to be a part of a Revolution that's way too big to fit on a bumper sticker.

Once you've made it through the maze of Jesus fish stickers and angel figurines and actually get to the Bible section, you're probably going to be just as overwhelmed. It's a staggering array. I heard that the head of one of the Bible publishing houses said their goal was to have every Christian purchase twenty-six Bibles in his or her lifetime. And the publishers are making sure that they have enough product lines to make that a reality.

In his book *Your God Is Too Safe*, Mark Buchanan describes the ridiculous profusion of specialty Bibles:

> We have every translation of the Bible you can imagine—the NIV, the NEV, the KJV, the NKJV, the NASV, the NRSAV, the Preacher's Bible, the Worshipper's Bible, the Spirit-Filled Believer's Bible, the left-handed bald gypsy fiddler's Bible, with versions for the nearsighted and the farsighted. (That last was made up.)[4]

Some of the extras in those specialty Bibles can be helpful, and I'm not saying you should avoid them. But they aren't essential,

4. Mark Buchanan, *Your God Is Too Safe: Rediscovering the Wonder of a God You Can't Control* (Sisters, OR: Multnomah, 2001), 200.

and they make for a more expensive product. You can find Bibles for just a few bucks, especially on the Internet. Or you can come to our church in Cincinnati, and we'll give you one for free.

You're still probably asking, "But which version is really the best?" Some translations are more "word-for-word" accurate than other translations. Some are more easily readable. At this point in your spiritual formation, however, any translation will work. A lot of people have a copy of the King James Version (KJV) lying around, often a family heirloom or taken from the hotel nightstand (thanks, Gideon Bible-givers). The KJV is a trusty old workhorse, but it's going to be hard for you to hang with a language style that you don't actually use in everyday conversation. I highly encourage you to get yourself a translation that doesn't have *thees*, *thous*, and *whithers*.

I don't know everything, but I do know this: the best version is the one you will actually read. The important thing right now is that you develop the discipline of reading your Bible. If you are reading your Bible on a regular basis and you understand it, then stay with it. If you find yourself wanting a change to bring some freshness to your reading, then go buy another one. In fact, if you want to buy twenty-six Bibles in your lifetime, that's great. Just make sure you actually read them and do what they say.

And before I start talking about some ways to get into the Bible, let's talk about some handling instructions. Remember when you were a grade-schooler and the librarian told you never to bend a corner of the book? That's a good rule for when a book's going to be used by hundreds of people, but when a book is yours and you want to get the most out of it, the "don't bend" law doesn't apply.

If I ever see you reading this book outside of Starbucks, I would be honored if the corners of the pages were creased. I hope to see notes scribbled in the margins. It would be great if highlighter bled from one page to the other. Marking up this book isn't a sign of rudeness; it's a sign of usefulness. This book is here to be used. The same goes with the Bible. God is honored when you mark it up because you are marking a moment of a lesson that you are intending on using.

The Bible is just a book until it gets used. The power of the Spirit comes into play when you embrace something that you just read and then actually do it. The truths of the Bible need to be embraced, not just the pages of the Bible.

When interacting with someone, I'll frequently realize that there's a truth in the Bible they need to not only know about, but embrace, meditate on, and apply. In cases like that, I'll actually grab the Bible closest to me and rip out the page that has the verse that the Spirit wants that person to live by. For instance, very few of my Bibles have the page where Romans 8:1 is located. (That's because so many people live in shame and guilt over past things that God has already forgiven them of. They—and you—need to know that "There is no condemnation for those who have a relationship with Jesus.") So . . . out comes the page with Romans 8:1.

BUT WHERE DO I START?

So you're sitting there with your Bible, and one of the first things that must be going through your mind is, *This is a big book. Where do I start?* I don't recommend starting at the beginning and just plowing through. You might make it through Genesis and Exodus, the first two books of the Bible, but then you're going to hit Leviticus, and you'll burn out. I guarantee it.

There is a reason for everything in the Bible, but that doesn't mean you'll benefit from everything in the stage you are in right now. So, if you come to one of those sections that has a page or two of genealogies, I recommend you skip over them. If you don't, you're likely to just zone out. Then you'll feel guilty that you've let your mind wander and wasted time, and you'll be tempted to go back and try it again. Don't do that. You'll probably just zone out again, and eventually you'll give up altogether.

You need a reading strategy that will help you get into the habit of reading and give you some momentum. You need to start with books of the Bible that are easier to read and that *have immediate impact on your life.* The reading strategy I'm about to lay out will give you some grounding as to who Jesus is and what the Bible is all about. Then you'll have a great foundation when you venture into other parts of it.

So here's how I recommend tackling the Bible:

1) READ THE BOOK OF JOHN.

The book of John (sometimes called "the gospel of John") is the best book in the Bible for communicating who Jesus is and the impact that truth can have on your life. You'll be exposed to some of Jesus' miracles and teachings, and you'll encounter people who are very similar to you. *Note: There are some short books close to the end of the Bible called 1 John, 2 John, and 3 John. Those are letters written by the apostle John, and they're great for quick-accomplishment junkies. But I'm talking about the longer book, the fourth book of the New Testament.*

READ THE BOOK OF JOHN AGAIN.

By going right back to this book and reading it again, you will gain insights you missed the first time around. This isn't just because you zoned (well, sometimes it is), but because God's Word is "living and active. Sharper than any double-edged sword."[5] It's like looking at the sky; you think you know what it looks like, but it's very dynamic, always changing. As many times as I've read the Bible through (some verses I bet I've read a hundred times), I'm still struck by how often I see something I never saw before.

2) READ EPHESIANS.

This is an example of an epistle—a letter written by one of Jesus' apostles to members of the early church. Ephesians has some great applications for how to live life in the here and now. One of my favorite sections in the Bible is Ephesians 6. Seeing life as a spiritual battle will probably help you make sense of things you've already noticed.

3) READ GENESIS.

This is the first book of the Bible and will be a great way to ease yourself into the Old Testament. There is a reason why this is the first book. It is because the truths contained here are the foundation

---

Spiritual Warfare: the fight between God, Satan, and their forces (angels and demons, respectively) for control over us. The fight is not visible to the naked eye. What is visible are the ramifications: racism and resolution, poverty and generosity, violence and peace, hatred and love.

---

5. Hebrews 4:12

on which the Bible builds. You might get stuck after chapter 1 because you will be forced to wrestle with theistic creation, atheistic evolution, or some hybrid. This is sure to be one of the accounts that is either hard to read or hard to understand, but it's time for you to begin wrestling with some of these issues. At some point you'll need to find resources from biblical scholars that shed light on this debate—light that the schools you attended probably failed to shed.

4) READ ROMANS.

This is another epistle. Here you'll find the apostle Paul writing to Christ-followers in Rome about what it means to have a life devoted to God. Rome has much in common with our modern society; therefore we have much to learn from what Paul wrote.

6) MEANWHILE, BE READING PSALMS AND PROVERBS.

While you are reading the above, I recommend having a daily goal of reading a few verses from Proverbs and a chapter from the book of Psalms. If you want to read more, do it. If you want to read less, that's fine too. You are in growth mode, and you don't need to be concerned about doing it all right away. Remember, growth is gradual and growth is intentional. The important thing is the journey, not the destination.

By reading Proverbs you will get immediate insights into how to survive and thrive in this life. The truths of Proverbs are practical, doable, and sensible. The life advice you receive will further reinforce the reliability of God's Word.

Psalms is important because it models for you what a prayer life looks like. King David wrote most of the psalms. They are a record of how he poured out his heart before God with incredible honesty—which means he doesn't always say the "right" thing.

You'll be surprised at how often he tells God things you've thought yourself but felt you weren't supposed to say. David reflects on things that have made his life better (Psalm 1). He reflects on things that have brought pain to his life (Psalm 51). He vents with God over things that tick him off (Psalm 52). These chapters will model for you what real prayer and a real relationship with God are all about.

A FEW ROADBLOCKS

When you start reading the Bible, you're probably going to have some thoughts and feelings that you think you shouldn't have. You'll get bored. You'll read things that make you mad. You'll have doubts. I want to reassure you: all of that is perfectly normal. It doesn't mean you're a bad person or a bad Christ-follower. So let me give you some strategies for dealing with each of these "rebellious" thoughts and feelings.

"I'M BORED."

You're reading along in your Bible, and a thought begins sneaking up on you: *I'm bored. This has nothing to do with me.* You feel guilty for thinking such a thing, but you just can't help it. It's as if the words you're reading were written for somebody else. Sometimes I feel that way too.

One thing to remember about the Bible is that even though it looks like a book, it's really a library. It's a collection of sixty-six books written to different people over the course of several centuries. All sixty-six books point to God and come from God, but they do it in different ways, in different styles, ranging from poetry to letters to history to prophecy. When I walk into a library,

I know there's a lot of truth on the shelves. But some of it just isn't helpful to me where I am at the moment. Some of what is on the shelves of the Bible may not be helpful to you, especially at this point in your spiritual life. No need to go near Deuteronomy right now. And please stay away from Revelation too. At this stage, it will only be confusing and give you crazy nightmares.

The Bible is God's love letter to you, but it is also written to a lot of different people, and it covers a lot of things that you aren't going to find the slightest bit interesting at a given moment. That's okay. As you mature, you will realize that some things you thought were throwaways turn out to be totally relevant to your life. In this, your earliest stage of the Revolution, I recommend that you skip the parts of the Bible that seem boring or irrelevant. You can come back to those parts later—maybe many years later—when you're ready for them.

It's important to remember that the Bible isn't God. It reveals who God is. It is never wrong. But it isn't God. God won't be mad if you choose to skip to a section that is speaking more to where you are right now. The most important thing is to have God breathing into you through His Word. Don't worry if some words aren't doing it. Keep going until you find some that do.

"I DON'T LIKE WHAT I'M SEEING IN THE BIBLE."

Sometimes people have the idea that if you're a "good" follower of Jesus, you're going to like everything He tells you to do. You won't. You're going to read things in the Bible that make you mad. You're going to discover that God does things differently from the way you would do things if you were God.

The good news of the Bible is that God loves you and wants what is best for you. In fact, He loves you so much that He became a man and died for your sake so you could get back the life that sin had made impossible. But "God loves me" and "I like everything about God" are two different things altogether.

We come to the Bible hoping it will confirm our best wishes. But because of the Fall, we aren't very good at knowing what to wish for. A transformed life lines itself up with God's truth. Unfortunately, we are inclined not to like the truth when we see it. That's a big part of what the Fall means.

The Bible says all sorts of things that are "backward" and unpopular. So how has it survived all these centuries? Why is it the best-selling book in the history of the world? Because it's true and its truth works. There are a lot of things that I've read or learned that I never liked, but they still work. I don't like the fact of gravity. I don't like the broken bones I've had as a result of gravity. Nonetheless, gravity is there, and it works. If I recognize it and don't fight against it, my life will be better for it.

I can't remember ever regretting a single thing I've done that the Bible told me to do. On the other hand, I can remember numerous times I've gotten myself in trouble because I ignored what God instructed in His love letter. He doesn't want to constrict me. He wants to give me freedom. The more I know Him and His ways and then follow Him and His ways, the more freedom I'll experience.

God is a healthy leader who gets no joy out of simply telling you what to do. He gets joy from your relationship with Him and seeing you build the kind of life that works. By giving you clear instructions, He is minimizing the pain you will cause for yourself and maximizing the peace you will experience in this life. He knows how this life works.

I don't like the fact, however, that God doesn't guarantee me a pain-free life. My dad is a nuclear engineer. He is the classic linear kind of guy. If A = B + C then C + B = A. I've inherited some of my dad's characteristics. I tend to assume that my relationship with Jesus will keep pain away from me. I tend to assume that when I live a moral life, God will keep calamity away from me. I tend to assume that doing acts of love will keep others from doing acts of hatred to me. Linear, right?

I don't like the fact that even though I'm writing a spiritual book and giving away a large percentage of my income and being a half-decent earthly father and not looking at Internet porn, I still could be diagnosed with cancer tomorrow. All my children could be killed in a car accident this afternoon.

I know this because I just read the book of Job in the Bible—and I didn't like it a bit. Job did everything by the book. Yet, for whatever reason, God allowed him to lose his health, his wealth, and his family. All of it—gone. I don't like the book of Job at all. Except that it's true. There's a reason God included it in His love letter to us. When I let go of my resentment, the book of Job begins to speak to me. It tells me that when things go wrong in my life, it might not be my fault. It tells me to stop beating myself up and to surrender to God. These are truths that wouldn't have been available to me if the Bible had told me what I wanted to hear about suffering. You've heard me use that word "surrender" before. If God only told us what we wanted to hear, where would the surrender be?

Our first reaction when we see something we don't like in the Bible is to doubt that it's true. That's what spiritual midgets do. Spiritual midgets are people who think more highly of themselves than they should.[6] Spiritual midgets think they have all the answers to the spiritual life. In reality, when we don't like something, it might be a sign from God that He is about to grow us.

---

6. Romans 12:3

I like things that comfort me, things I have mastered or at least have some control over. For example, I like reading articles about physical health when I've been working out and eating healthy. In other words, I most enjoy health-related articles when I need them least. On the other hand, those things I don't like or am discomforted by are those things I haven't figured out or am not doing. Reading about those things convicts me and makes me feel powerless—and this is exactly where God wants me. It is in His power that we find true comfort, not in our delusions of being in control.

A couple of pages back, I gave you permission to skip those parts of the Bible that you find boring or irrelevant. However, when you come to a part of the Bible that you don't like, do just the opposite. Stay there for a while. Sit in it. You'll be amazed at what God does in your life.

"How can I know that these really are God's words and not just the ideas of a bunch of guys who have been dead for thousands of years?"

It's not just spiritual midgets who have doubts about the truth of the Bible. I'm the first to admit it: it's hard to believe that this collection of sixty-six books penned by dozens of different people in two different languages could truly be God's Word. It's hard to believe, but I believe it. It's hard to believe that the human eye could actually work. It's hard to believe where babies come from. It's hard to believe the Bengals have never won a Super Bowl . . . okay, not really. But I believe all those things. And I believe that the people who penned the various parts of the Bible were under the supernatural influence of God. Those writers' personalities and writing styles came out in the document, but the message and truth contained therein come directly from the heart and mind of God.

There are several ways to approach the question of the Bible's veracity. We could talk about it historically. In about AD 325, the most respected leaders in Christianity came together and said to one another, "We need to nail down who was inspired by God when they wrote and who wasn't." This was a simpler exercise than you might think, because people had been making hand copies for centuries, and the cream had risen to the top. By AD 190 there was near-consensus about what was from God and what wasn't. Furthermore, there were thousands and thousands of copies, which made it easier to determine which was the original. If you only have two copies, you have a 50/50 chance of knowing which has the right wording. Today archaeology has unearthed no fewer than 45,000 early handwritten manuscripts. That gives us a very high degree of confidence that the words you read line up with the original.

With all the television coverage, new books, and recent magazine articles, you may be thinking, *What about all the lost books of the Bible?* There are no lost books. There are discarded books. There are books that no one chose to copy because they weren't worth anything, so they were pitched. Think about it this way: in two thousand years, people may dig up an old supermarket site and find documentation that says an alien boy with a snake head was found in a local hospital. That doesn't mean it's true; it means the *National Enquirer* was trying to sell newspapers with stories that rational, well-educated people didn't take seriously. But if you think Jesus used to put curses on people, or made inanimate objects fly to impress his friends, or actually said that until a woman literally becomes a man she's worthless,[7] then you'll love the "lost gospels." For the rest of us, stick with the

---

7. Gospel of Thomas 114: Simon Peter said to them, "Let Mary leave us, for women are not worthy of life." Jesus said, "I myself shall lead her in order to make her male, so that she too may become a living spirit resembling you males. For every woman who will make herself male will enter the kingdom of heaven."

authorized biographies of Matthew, Mark, Luke, and John. They are real, and they work.

In speaking for itself, the Bible says this:

> And we have the word of the prophets made more certain, and you will do well to pay attention to it, as to a light shining in a dark place, until the day dawns and the morning star rises in your hearts. Above all, you must understand that no prophecy of Scripture came about by the prophet's own interpretation. For prophecy never had its origin in the will of man, but men spoke from God as they were carried along by the Holy Spirit.[8]

Being "carried along by the Holy Spirit" is another way of saying that Scripture is "God-breathed." Remember 2 Timothy 3:16–17? When you hold a Bible, you don't have in your hands just human understanding. You have God's understanding on every matter to which the Book speaks. The Bible isn't somebody's interpretation. It is God's revelation of how He is to be known and how you should live your life. No person willed the Bible into being. It was breathed into being while humans were carried along by God's guidance.

But the truth is, if you don't believe the Bible is the Word of God, you can't really take its claims for itself as being authoritative. And you probably aren't all that impressed by a gathering of church leaders in AD 325.

So where does that leave you?

One claim the Bible makes for itself is that it is "living and active" and "sharper than any double-edged sword."[9] That's a claim you can test—but only if you engage the Bible on a personal

---

8. 2 Peter 1:19–21
9. Hebrews 4:12

level. Don't take my word for it. Actually, do take my word for it, but only temporarily. Start reading the Bible every day, and see for yourself what happens. And while you're reading or before you read, ask God to make it clear to you what message He wants you to hear.

You will see what it means to say that this book is "living and active." The Spirit who inspired the Bible will begin to stir inside of you—and the academic exercise of "proving" that the Bible is true or untrue will seem strangely irrelevant. Sometimes you hear people talk about a book "coming alive." If you get in the habit of reading the Bible and applying its truths to your life, you will come alive. And that's the real proof that the Bible is God's Word.

I've been reading the Bible for a long time, and I have to say that I'm a little jealous of you. I would love to go back into the Bible and read stories again without knowing how they end. And I wish I could read the Bible without having a bias from the many preachers, teachers, and professors who have influenced my thinking. Don't get me wrong. We all need instruction from people who know more than we do. But there is nothing like experiencing the teachings and life-altering stories of the Bible for the first time. Oftentimes, the thing that I was first taught wasn't the accurate interpretation but the safe interpretation. You have the opportunity to be taught by the Spirit of God as you read His Word without the baggage that many of us have. Relish your unique perspective. And enjoy what God is about to do in your life.

You know that Bible I told you to go get? Turn to the inside cover or the very first blank page and write, "Dear (Your Name)," Now go to the very end of the Bible and write:

Love,
God.

BIBLE:
LETTER FROM A REVOLUTIONARY

All went pretty well in my life (or so I thought) until I hit high school. I had grown up in the Southern Baptist Church, read the Bible through twice by the time I was ten, and had a fascination with God. Then, being the nerd that I am, I became a philosopher and outgrew my need for the crutch that I had come to believe God was. I buried myself in scientific explanations for and against the existence of a divine creator.

Eventually, and much to my chagrin, I had to be honest with myself and relent that there had to be a God. My reason is actually the proof that atheists use to "prove" there is no God: math. Modern science uses math to explain the origin of the cosmos and reality. It does a bang-up job of it. The current paradigm of quantum mechanics and big-bang theories very neatly and logically explains the spontaneous origination of the universe . . . up to a point. The formulas all work until one-millionth of one nanosecond before the big bang took place. At this point, all the smartest guys in the room give a collective shrug and change the subject.

So, I had come to the conclusion there was a God, but now the problem was which one was it? Buddha? Too wimpy. Baptist? Too militant. Catholic?

I'm not much of a gambler. Hindu? Too many arms. At this point I restarted my search. I read the Bible a few more times, looking for reasons Jesus wasn't the answer. I looked so much I got sick of it. I hated the idea of God, church, and faith. I had "progressed" to the other ugly "a" word . . . agnostic.

That all changed in 2006. My mother, father, best friend, and I were involved in a very serious car accident. After the wreck, but before being cut out, I had the subtle feeling that God was trying to get my attention. Within a month of that day, God brought someone into my life who really challenged me to seek Him again. That was the beginning of this process.

I have doubts and concerns and, in all likelihood, always will. However, Christ has done some truly astounding things in my life this past year—once I began to listen and surrender my own concerns. About six months ago, I opened my Bible again. Within two days I had largely overcome an addiction to pornography that I had fought and lost on a daily basis for most of my life. It turns out that as soon as I quit pushing my questions and simply allowed God to speak, I got more answers than I could have expected.

PRAYER

PART I: BEING WITH GOD

When I was a kid, Thanksgiving was the most awkward of all holidays. I spent the fourth Thursday of every November with the other kids at the "nobody" table—the card table just off the dining room for those of us who didn't have the seniority to sit with the older people at the "somebody" table. And the only way to move up was for a somebody to die or divorce. We could see them. We could hear snatches of their conversations. But there wasn't any significant interaction except when one of the somebodies scolded us for doing something they didn't like.

The most cringy moment of the whole day, however, came when a somebody was recruited to mumble grace over the food. I remember sitting at that rickety, "nobody" card table asking myself questions like, *Why do they keep saying "thee" and "thou"? Why do they pray before this meal when they don't before the others? For that matter, why do some of these people pray at all? I never hear them talk about God any other time. Most of them only go to church if somebody dies.*

Ah, the innocence of childhood. Children see things simply—

and often more truthfully—than the rest of us. Kids can smell pretense and indifference from five playgrounds away.

If you're going to be a part of the Revolution, prayer is key. But not the kind of prayer I witnessed at the Thanksgivings of my youth. Not ceremonial religious babble. Not holy talk designed to impress others or memorized incantations that have no personal meaning. Prayer is relational connection. Prayer is being with God and asking for things to be different. It is trusting that He can change the physical and spiritual world and, in the process, send down His warrior angels. If the chance to relate to God in this way doesn't blow your mind—if you can't see the intense power in that—go back to prayer beads and boring Thanksgivings. But if you want more, you can have it.

We don't *have* to pray. We *get* to pray. God invites us into a loving relationship in which He welcomes our questions, requests, and statements. But prayer is even more than that. God wants us to communicate *with* Him, not just talk *at* Him. Communication means that I am telling God exactly what I'm thinking, explaining what I need and feel and hope for, and then receiving His answers. Answers of calm, answers of healing, answers that kick your butt into gear. That's healthy communication: it goes in two directions. You talk, God talks; you respond, God responds.

Imagine that you could take Jesus to happy hour or grab coffee together before your day starts. You wouldn't just go, stare straight ahead, and waste time. You'd admit things, vent, laugh, question each other, and explore new ideas. You'd tell Him about the hurtful thing your dad said, how you need to be saved from an affair, what you'd love to have happen tomorrow. You'd be like, "Hey, Jesus, come on . . . One more drink," and then you'd ask if He thinks your new jeans make you look fat. (He'd probably say no to the drink and yes to the jeans.)

That's what you get to have. That's what it's like to have healthy, exciting, life-and-world-changing communication. That's what it means to live together with Jesus.

And here's something crucial that you might not know, something that religious systems sometimes forget to clue you in on: Prayer isn't just about you and God. Prayer is about the Revolution. Prayer is about bringing the Kingdom to Earth and working with God to change the world for other people.

Maybe this is a hard thing for people to believe—that our prayers matter beyond ourselves, that we can ask and receive and create huge change. But we can. Our prayer *does* motivate God to send down His spiritual forces. Our prayer *does* call down the heavens. Look how Jesus did it: time and again the Bible records that He "went away to pray." He left the immediate demands and pressures that were before Him and escaped to interact with His heavenly Father. He didn't pray out of obligation. He seized it as an opportunity to increase His spiritual power and change everything around Him.

CREATE SPACE

Now you know the potential of prayer, but you should also know that you've got to have a plan, because otherwise prayer just falls into our leftover minutes before bedtime, or we forget about it altogether and the spiritual forces remain at the ready, holding back, waiting to be unleashed.

Nothing healthy happens without a plan. Children aren't their healthiest without a devoted parent who consistently disciplines and affirms. Bodies aren't healthy without a plan for exercise, rest, and nutrition. Gardens look pathetic if you don't weed and water.

All healthy things require an ongoing plan that includes structures for tangible action, not just lofty ideals.

What does this look like? Jesus describes a way to get into communication with God:

> When you pray, go into your room, close the door and pray to your Father, who is unseen . . . And when you pray, do not keep on babbling like pagans, for they think they will be heard because of their many words. Do not be like them, for your Father knows what you need before you ask him.[1]

Jesus is telling us to create space: make time ("when you pray"), make a place ("go into your room"), and make it simple ("do not keep babbling like pagans"). Let's take a closer look at that.

Don't just make a goal to "pray more." A general goal to pray more won't work any more than a general goal to lose weight or get out of debt. Goals that work are the ones linked with a specific plan. To lose weight, you need a plan that includes eating fewer calories and working out for a certain amount of time every week. To get out of debt, you need a plan to pay a set amount of money to your creditors and eliminate credit card spending.

In the same way, you need preplanned times for prayer. There's no time limit on how often we should pray. Nor is there necessarily one time that's a more spiritual time than another. In fact, the Bible tells us to "pray at all times without ceasing."[2] But you need to set a cornerstone time on which everything else builds.

For me, this time is first thing in the morning before I get into the office. If I don't make that time—which includes getting to bed at a decent hour the night before—significant prayer won't happen.

---

1. Matthew 6:6–8
2. 1 Thessalonians 5:17, paraphrased

You need to figure out what time you are going to connect with God, intentionally schedule it, and then keep the appointment.

How much time you need depends on a number of factors. If you go from not praying at all to scheduling five minutes a day for communication with God, you are five minutes closer to having the kind of life He wants to share with you. Hopefully you'll build from there, but it's a start—and nothing to be ashamed of. Wherever you are right now, proactively make time to communicate.

MARK A SPOT

Jesus says that when we pray, we should go into a room and pray. What room is He talking about? It's any room you choose, any physical space that you've set aside for prayer. Make a daily appointment with God, at a certain location, in the same way you do with other people who matter to you.

In the Tome family, when we drive our kids to school, we pray for a blessing on their teachers and for a day of safety. We also pray for an increased aptitude for them to be able to learn. We usually pray at the light of a particular corner gas station. One time I started praying a few blocks early, and all my kids immediately got annoyed and said, "No, Dad."

"It doesn't matter where we pray," I said. I was about to play the extra-spiritual card, but they interrupted me again.

"That's not the way we do it, Dad."

Some patterns can be good and helpful. That corner is a sort of holy ground for our kids. It is important to stake out holy ground, to have a place that is reserved for one-on-one time with God, a place away from the public eye. We need to go to our own place and shut the door. This helps us to focus, and it sends a signal to ourselves and to God that we have a purpose right now—and that purpose is to connect and communicate with our Creator.

Every place I've lived since I've been a follower of Jesus, I have marked off a spot for my daily, intentional time with God. These places aren't off-limits to others. They are just off-limits to me unless I'm communing with God. It sets up a trigger. A trigger is any object, event, or action that stimulates a reaction. So when you hear the music from *Jaws*, you automatically think about shark attacks. Every time. You could be on the top of Mount Everest, but if you hear "da-DUM . . . da-DUM . . . daDUM daDUM daDUM," yeah, you're gonna cringe.

A friend of mine has a history of going into a porn superstore on a stretch of highway several hours from his home. Every month he drives by the place on his way to his hometown, and often he finds himself instinctively pulling into the parking lot even though he has made a specific goal to never go there again. Seeing that place is a trigger for him. Even though he has a choice, the trigger makes it really difficult to follow through on his commitments.

Just as you can avoid negative triggers, you can create positive ones for your own good. You can approach prayer this way. For instance, there's one end of the couch in the small second-story den in our house where I sit only when I'm interacting with God. There I sit and read the Bible, pray, journal, reflect. I only use the space in front of that spot when I'm kneeling and confessing the sin in my life. If I'm in that room talking with someone, I make sure I'm sitting on the other side of the couch. The side by the lamp is where I talk with God and He talks with me. It's my trigger for intimate spiritual things.

Think of a place right now that would work for you. Now choose a time. Now commit.

MAKE IT SIMPLE

Prayer is a personal conversation. That's all. If someone tries to convince you that you need to go through a bunch of spiritual or mystical gymnastics, take that person as someone who's just putting on a show.

Jesus said, "Do not keep babbling on like pagans." What's a pagan? A person who doesn't make God smile. Pagans aren't necessarily atheists or drug dealers or mothers-in-law. The category encompasses a lot of people who are ultrareligious. Religious people who memorize certain phrases, use flowery sayings, and sound impressive in public. But that doesn't mean they're connecting with God. They are communicating something, but they aren't praying. They are communicating that they don't know God well enough to actually talk to Him personally. When we "babble," as Jesus puts it, we are using extravagant and repetitive verbiage for the sake of other people, not for the sake of our relationship with God.

You don't babble at people you know intimately. Do you know when I start babbling? I babble at parties where I don't know people very well. I can get very animated. I talk a little louder. I end up talking about the same things over and over. I ask someone's name. I talk about the weather. I talk about the lead stories in the news. I ask their name again because I didn't listen the first time. I babble because I don't know what to say, because I'm nervous, because I don't want to be real with people I don't really know.

But if I really know you, I talk differently. I speak very simply. I tell you about my nasties. I don't try to use long words or interesting grammar the way I do when I'm talking to a stranger. With good friends, sometimes I just scratch myself and grunt. A simple grunt can say a lot.

Ironically, people who are still seeking God often have a more powerful prayer life than people who have been around long enough to learn all the stock phrases. Seekers often don't know any better than to communicate with God in the same language they would communicate with anybody else. Seekers talk to God like this: "Help. I need to figure out if You are really there, God. I think that You want us to be in a relationship. Help me understand who You are. God, I know You care about people who are hurting. Well, I'm hurting. Please help me figure out how I should deal with Tom, who keeps riding my butt."

That is the kind of prayer God listens to—a prayer that is simple and speaks our hearts. Don't bother saying what you don't mean or feel. "Many words" don't impress God. They only frustrate Him because they aren't authentic. He knows we've got deeper things to say. He knows we've got anger, questions, passions, stories about our day. Give Him that stuff. Tell it like it is.

ONE METHOD FOR PRAYER

So how, exactly, do you pray? Hey, I'm not falling for that one. There's no "exact" way to pray. I'm willing to give you one format for prayer, but you've got to receive it in the spirit in which I give it. I'm not trying to give you a rigid formula that you should always follow. I'm just trying to get you started. Sometimes it helps to have a guideline to follow, a guideline that covers the basics and gives you a platform to jump from. So here's my suggested format: PRAY—Praise, Repent, Ask, Yield. (I'm always a sucker for acronyms.)

Praise

We all like being thanked and complimented, and so does God. This should be an easy task, given how many incredible things

He has done in you and for you. Thank Him for the way He forgives you, His mercy over your mistakes, His justice, His power. Thank Him for how these characteristics specifically matter to your life.

Everybody praises something. It's just the way we're made. Something captures your mind, something gives you enjoyment, and you can't help but put your pleasure into words. "Mmm, that pie is good!" "That's a sweet ride!" "You are my sunshine, my only sunshine. You make me happy, when skies are gray." (Is that weird?) Praise just comes out of you, sometimes involuntarily. When you're really into someone you're dating, you can hardly help but tell them how great they are and how much they mean to you. When your team scores, you shout out praise and adoration. Grown men, beers in hand, get misty-eyed as they scream at the TV, "You da man! I love you!" Praise simply happens naturally.

We praise God because He is worth it. You're going to praise something, so why not praise the One who is truly worthy of it? Where your heart is, that's where your treasure will be.[3] Praise helps you to value that which is truly valuable.

A big part of praise is expressing your gratitude—not just in a general sense, but specifically. As you've probably experienced, the more specific people are when voicing their appreciation for you, the more you believe what they're saying; you don't just dismiss it as false praise or brownnosing. Being told "You did a good job" isn't nearly as meaningful as "I noticed how you stayed late for that project and how you listened to other people's input. Your great work ethic, coupled with the ability to value others on the team, is one of the things that sets you apart in this company. I'm glad I work with you." If your boss says that, you are floating home.

---

3. Matthew 6:21, paraphrased

WELCOME TO THE REVOLUTION

It's impossible to have a good relationship with anybody without expressing gratitude. And when we express genuine gratitude and goodwill, it doesn't carry with it the expectation that the person needs to change or improve. Gratitude is sincere.

If you haven't noticed already, one of the ways I continually praise God is by capitalizing any reference to Him. This gives me a subtle reminder that there is a God—and I'm not Him. Every time I do this, He is taking some pleasure in my small act of praise and awe, and my spirit is becoming more like the image of Jesus.

God doesn't need any pointers. He only needs praise. This is how the Bible puts it:

> Every good and perfect gift is from above, coming down from the Father of the heavenly lights, who does not change like shifting shadows.[4]

Without question, there are things in your life that are not "good" and definitely not "perfect." (Remember the Fall and what we brought upon ourselves?) And yet the Bible tells us to rejoice even during painful times. It may be hard for you to resist assigning some blame to God for the problems in your life. Perhaps that lack of gratitude is what keeps you from having a powerful prayer life. Yes, bring your problems to God to be dealt with, but remember the foundation for your prayer life is praise. You wouldn't have any of those problems if God hadn't given you life.

Stop reading and take a moment to praise God right now. Maybe you've never done this before. Just think about your life this year and thank Him for something specific that has been taking place that you think He has a hand in. (He has.)

---

4. James 1:17

REPENT

After you've praised God for who He is and what He's done, it's time to recognize your own shortcomings. As a matter of fact, having recognized God's greatness makes it easy to recognize your own pettiness. To do this is to repent. Repenting is recognizing our sin and then resolving to take responsibility for it. Taking responsibility includes asking for forgiveness, trying to make the situation right, and not repeating the same mistake.

Repentance means turning around and going in a different direction. It's abrupt. It's like when food poisoning hits, and you can't even make it two minutes away from the table before you publicly display that the last bite was a mistake.

> **Repentance:** the decision to change your mind, attitude, and behavior in relationship to a sinful thing in which you've participated.

Remember the story from the last chapter about the guys who ignored all warning signs and drove off into the river? Those guys needed to repent. They needed to abruptly change direction. Instead, their self-will came into tragic conflict with the laws of gravity—a force that they could not overcome.

Repentance is recognizing that we cannot overcome God. No matter how selfish we are or how stubborn we may be or how skilled we are at fooling others, we can't overcome the power of God.

When we recognize that there's no point in trying to change God's standards or blame God, we set about the work of trying to change ourselves. We begin the journey of repentance and restoration by giving Him simple words like, "I'm sorry for lying on my tax return. Please forgive me." "I'm sorry for having too much to drink last night. I realize I made myself look like an idiot, and I dishonored You in the process." "I'm sorry that yet again I've gossiped about somebody and taken the credit for what the whole team did. Please forgive me." "I'm really sorry for stealing photos from that Florida resort with the pathetic and stingy customer service." (Okay, so I'm not quite over it.)

But seriously, when you say things like that to God, you're on your way to increased spiritual power. You've acknowledged your mistakes—you've gotten them out of darkness—and that begins the change. Private sin that you haven't dealt with will kill your prayer life quicker than anything else.

When I broke my arm in first grade, the doctor told me that when it healed, my arm would actually be stronger in that place than it was before. When we become broken over our sin and repent, we actually become stronger than we were before. God's healing power comes into us and strengthens us beyond where we were in the first place. Why? Two things happen. One: something that was counterfeit (against the Kingdom) gets smashed because it comes out into the light. Two: the healed area is thicker, more protected, than it was before.

For this to happen, however, repentance needs to go beyond a simple "I'm sorry" in your morning prayers. The Bible says, "Therefore confess your sins to each other and pray for each other so that you may be healed. The prayer of a righteous man is powerful and effective" (James 5:16).

Here we can see again how the three-legged stool of spiritual formation works. The Bible is instructing us on one of the finer points of repentance: confession to another person. This is a key component of community. You don't need to go to a religious professional to ask for forgiveness. You can go to any safe follower of Christ (we'll talk more about safe people in the next chapter).

Going to somebody else will give you a sense of healing; the result is a power that you won't get if you just keep it between you and God. Think of it as a way of moving your prayer of repentance out into the larger world, thereby rebuilding and strengthening yourself—and probably strengthening others at the same time.

When we confess and repent, relationships are restored, although sometimes that restoration involves hard work and discipline. Of course, the most important relationship that is restored is our relationship with God. And again, this relational connection is the foundation for powerful and effective prayer.

ASK

Now we have the foundation for the fun part. Let's ask God for some stuff. There's nothing sacrilegious about that. You don't want to be one of those people who feels guilty or unworthy of asking God for anything. If you've seen "Wayne's World," you might remember the scene when Wayne and Garth go to see their hero Alice Cooper. As soon as they see him, they fall down on their knees and chant, "We're not worthy. We're not worthy." It's ridiculous and embarrassing. That's not how God wants you to approach Him. He wants you to approach Him boldly, confidently.

> Let us then approach the throne of grace with confidence, so
> that we may receive mercy and find grace to help us in our time
> of need.[5]

---

5. Hebrews 4:16

Listen to me very carefully. If you have decided to become part of God's family, you are worthy to ask God for anything. Anything. Plus, God really enjoys hearing your requests, and He likes it even more when there is a good reason to say yes.

> Ask and it will be given to you; seek and you will find; knock and the door will be opened to you. For everyone who asks receives; he who seeks finds; and to him who knocks, the door will be opened.
>
> Which of you, if his son asks for bread, will give him a stone? Or if he asks for a fish, will give him a snake? If you, then, though you are evil, know how to give good gifts to your children, how much more will your Father in heaven give good gifts to those who ask him![6]

That's Jesus talking. The effort we make toward God has positive results; God honors it. Asking results in getting. Seeking results in finding. *Knocking* results in opening. God doesn't give us things we ask for if those things aren't good for us. He won't allow us to find something that we shouldn't be seeking, and He won't open a door that we shouldn't be knocking on.

Sometimes God's answer to your prayer is no. That's a very good thing, because it frees you up to ask for whatever's on your heart. You don't have to censor yourself—*I don't know . . . Should I ask for this, or should I not ask for it? What if it's the wrong thing?* If it's the wrong thing, God will give you a no. Pretty simple. And, when you think about it, pretty comforting. Mythology and folklore are full of stories of people who suffer horribly because they could have anything they wished for, and the gods couldn't say no. Think of poor Midas. He wished that everything he touched

---

6. Matthew 7:7–11

would turn to gold. He got his wish, and it made him very happy. Until he touched his supper and realized it's hard to digest a golden pork chop. Until he touched his beloved daughter and turned her into a golden girl. But the Bible doesn't tell that kind of horror story. Because God doesn't mind saying no.

So ask boldly. God delights in giving good things to His children. Even bad earthly fathers will give occasional good gifts. How much more will God!

In asking, we need to be specific. If you have a sick friend, don't address God by saying, "I pray for John" and leave it at that. What does "I pray for . . ." mean? It's a statement, not a request. How about, "God, would you please heal John? He's sick, and I'm worried about him." No wonder our prayer life can be frustrating; we mumble things that aren't even prayers and can't be answered. As Billy Graham said, "Heaven is full of answers to prayers for which no one ever bothered to ask."[7]

One of the most powerful examples of prayer in my life was when I was a part of a community of people praying that God would help us buy a lumber warehouse for our church to leverage in pursuing our mission. About thirty of us gathered in the parking lot of a local Home Quarters warehouse to pray for the upcoming auction of the building. We specifically asked God to allow us to buy it with the amount of money we had (which was $4.6 million) and to "blind and confuse" the competitors who had more resources than we did.

That was a special time of prayer as we leveraged the power of praying in community. We also leveraged a story from the Bible (remember the three-legged stool?) where Joshua led the people of Israel on a march around the city of Jericho seven times prior to invasion and victory. So as we stood in the front

---

7. Billy Graham, Till Armageddon: A Perspective on Suffering (London: Hodder & Stoughton, 1983) 153.

parking lot of the store, my daughter Lena said, "Daddy, how about we march around HQ?"

It seemed like a good idea to me, so I announced, "Friends, let's walk around this place seven times and ask for God to give it to us. Let's do it in silence as the Israelites did." So off we went. Just thirty people—and most of us didn't have any background in public prayer, since our church is made up of seekers and new followers of Christ.

I never realized how big that place was. We were all huffing and puffing, so we kept close to the building. What was especially challenging was coming around to the front of the building and walking past all the automatic doors. The building was still open during the liquidation sale. You could tell that all the employees were starting to wonder what thirty wackos were doing walking in circles around the building.

Well, we had something to ask God.

YIELD

Prayer, as I said earlier, is two-way communication. So once you've made your requests to God, it's time to get quiet and listen. I call it "yielding." Yielding is when you put your hands in the air and say, "Yeah, I surrender." When you're in a posture of submission, you can do nothing but wait for the One in authority to tell you what to do. You don't keep running your mouth. You shut up and wait for instructions.

This is when the communication becomes complete. God isn't interested in us hurrying through our grocery list— "I wanna new job and I wanna better house and I wanna hot date and I wanna raise and I wanna be rid of my zits and I wanna Red Ryder double-action-pump BB gun. Oh, and give us some world peace while you're at it"—and then getting on to the next item on our day's agenda.

God wants us to sincerely communicate with Him, and that means stopping and waiting for instructions. Be ready. God might ask you to repent of something you had forgotten about. He may move you to get up and go serve in some way. He might give you a peace and a confidence that you will get what you asked for. Who knows? He's God. He's not very predictable. In such times of quiet waiting, your thoughts might not actually be your thoughts. Your feelings might not be your feelings. Your impressions might not be your impressions. Instead, these thoughts, feelings, and impressions might be prompted by God. When you get one of these, follow through.

After our Jericho Walk, we debriefed, sharing our impressions with one another. People said they felt God's presence. They also sensed that the building would be ours. No one indicated that they thought there was anything else we needed to do or repent of which could have been a barrier to our getting a yes to our request.

Three days later I went to Manhattan for the auction of the building. I'll never forget standing in the lobby of a financial power center on Wall Street, weeping like a baby and rejoicing over the cell phone with the people back home: "God gave it to us. Isn't God good!"

We were able to buy the property—for exactly $4.6 million. We found out a week later that a major retailer was supposed to be there but had missed the flight to New York. They offered us $10 million. We have since discovered that two other deep-pocketed developers had their wires crossed and couldn't attend.

We paid what we had. God had literally blinded and confused those who stood in our way. God said, "Yes, that building is for you."

P. T. Forsyth is a spiritual hero from generations ago. He warned that the inability to pray is the punishment for the refusal to pray. No matter how short or crude your new prayer life may be, stay with it. Refuse to give up. God delights when He hears from you, and in time you'll learn His unique voice and thirst to hear it more.

BARRIERS TO PRAYER

If prayer is so simple, why do so few people actually do it? Because there are lots of barriers to prayer, and two of the biggest are insecurity and pride.

INSECURITY

For the first three years or so after I gave my life to Christ, I hardly ever prayed. Do you know why? I believed my life wasn't really all that important to God. I believed He would get bored. I thought that if I prayed too often, God would think, *What is this guy doing? Who does he think he is, Billy Graham? And who does he think I am, the speedy deliveryman? I don't have time for that kind of intensive personal service.*

I saved up my requests. That way, when I actually did spend time in prayer, God would say, "Hey, is that Brian Tome talking to me? If Brian Tome is talking to me, this must be serious. I better listen up and take some action!" Not only did this approach to prayer show how insecure I was, but it also showed how I was trying to work the system. But my understanding of the system was dead wrong.

I didn't realize that God revels in our relationship. I don't bore God. You don't bore Him either. He loves it when we communicate. If there's one book you should read on prayer, it's *Too Busy Not to Pray* by Bill Hybels. Bill has had a profound impact on my life; I'll never forget what he says in his book: "No one's voice sounds sweeter to God than yours."[8]

---

8. Bill Hybels, *Too Busy Not to Pray: Slowing Down to Be with God* (Downers Grove, IL: InterVarsity), 28.

That is true. God has created you, and He wants an open and vibrant relationship with you. All good parents want that. I want that with my children. During our nightly family dinnertimes, we have a tradition of taking turns telling the best and worst parts of our days. Some of those stories would bore you senseless, especially stories from when my kids were little and not quite clear on what constitutes an anecdote and what's just rambling. But those stories that would have bored you didn't bore me a bit. Those were my kids, after all, and just to hear them talk was music to my ears. In the same way, your voice is music to God's ears.

PRIDE

Prideful people eventually give up on prayer because they believe they can manage things on their own. They say (even if they don't say it out loud), "I don't need God on this one. I don't need God to help me choose my socks. I don't need God to get involved in my other commitments or aspirations." Unintentionally, yet unmistakably, they communicate to God, "I'm not interested in a relationship."

Where there is no relationship, there is no communication. Where there is no communication, there is pride. Where there is pride, there is pain just around the corner.

Sooner or later we all realize that we can't do life on our own. This normally happens as soon as we are faced with a significant crisis that a self-help seminar or a pharmaceutical product can't solve. So we pray—as the last resort. One key to spiritual growth is to pray as the first resort, not the last.

When we are faced with a big tragedy, our pride crumbles, and we realize that we really aren't in control. This happened with one of our country's greatest men, Abraham Lincoln. During the Civil War, the Union was suffering and losing many battles. Lincoln was being attacked by the press and facing intense pressure. Then at home, Lincoln's son unexpectedly died. And while Lincoln's wife looked for answers and comfort in spiritism, Lincoln turned to his Bible:

"My own wisdom seemed insufficient," he wrote to a friend. I was "driven many times upon my knees by the overwhelming conviction that I have nowhere else to go."[9]

"Nowhere else to go." That's where we all need to be, even when things are going our way. I've learned that I can do a lot of things without prayer. I just can't do anything of significance without prayer. There is nothing wrong with going to God in the crunch times, even if the crunch time has come about as a result of our sin or pride. In fact, God is using the crunch time to bring you into a better relationship with Him. Recognize, however, that there may be fewer crunch times if you give up your pride and turn to prayer.

PRAYER
PART II: PRAYING WITH YOUR IMAGINATION

Enough about methods and techniques for prayer and strategies for overcoming barriers. I offer them to help you begin a habit of praying, but you know from experience that when you're really close to another person, your communication isn't governed by conversational techniques or methods. It has more to do with the free flow of ideas and genuine engagement.

9. Quoted in "Lincoln's Spiritual Legacy" by Charles Colson, Breakpoint Ministry, p. 100.

I've found something that has transformed my prayer life by making my engagement with God deeper and more natural. My prayer life changed forever when I understood the value of using my imagination to connect with God. Stay with me here. It's not as kooky or as New Agey as it sounds. I'm not suggesting that God is an illusion or that you should talk to Him as if He were your imaginary friend. I'm talking about tapping into the truth that all planning, all understanding, all thought doesn't actually begin with words but with images.[10]

Somehow we've gotten the idea that prayer is a verbal exercise, all about putting requests and hopes and desires into literal words. That's part of it, of course. Putting your prayers into words—whether spoken or written in a journal—is one way of clarifying your own needs and hopes. But if prayer is a verbal exercise, that would make people who are good writers and good public speakers the spiritual elite; that would make them better at praying than everybody else. And that simply isn't the case.

I remember what a hard time I had with my college freshman English class. My instructor bled dry many a red ink pen on my six-hundred-word essays. I cringed even more when a new assignment was given out, thinking, *That ain't no how fair!*

Written communication isn't natural or fun for me. (Someone please remind me of this the next time I consider writing a book.) And for many of us, a bigger communication fear is speaking in public. According to psychologists, speaking in public is the number one fear that Americans have. So if talking to God primarily takes place through writing words or talking out loud, then most of us aren't going to do much speaking to Him.

You may not be good at making speeches or writing, but you

---

10. The best full treatment of this I've ever read is *Seeing is Believing* by Greg Boyd.

do have the inherent ability to imagine. It's one of the most fundamental things that separates us from monkeys. Before you say, "Actually, I'm not very imaginative," let me ask you a few questions. How do you plan? You imagine the future, then you work toward it. How do you relive pain and tragedy? You replay the pictures and scenes in slow motion through your memory.

Your imagination is the most powerful communication tool you possess. It is so powerful and so effortless that you use it without even thinking. It can create images crisper than HDTV, sounds as clear as surround sound, and has memory that works faster and lasts longer than any amount of RAM. This capacity was created by God.

What I'm suggesting is that your imagination exists not just to visualize the future or remember the past but also to pray for the future and to pray through the wounds of your past. I'm suggesting that God gave you imagination not so you could escape reality, but so you could create it! I'm suggesting that the most natural thing you do—imagine, fantasize, dream—is a gift from God to empower you to do the thing He most wants you to do: communicate with Him. But something about religion tells us that if something is easy and fun, then it must not count.

Many Christ-followers have a low view of imagination and therefore miss an entire realm that God has created and wants us to use in powerful ways. We shouldn't demean what God has created, yet we describe immature people as "very imaginative." We are concerned about school children who have an "overactive imagination" because we think they're not grounded in reality. People who can't hold down a job are described as "dreamers." But the imagination is something that God has created to be a blessing to us. For some reason, we "responsible adults" too often reject it. It's similar to our attitude toward sex. Sex is a beautiful,

God-given blessing—but it also carries danger with it, so "good Christians" try not to talk about it and end up with some pretty whacked ideas. Any good gift that God gives can be bastardized. But an equal danger is not using the gifts He gives in the way He intended them to be used.

Your mind's primary ability is to represent things through images and stories, not to craft grammatically correct sentences with no color, movement, or shape. So how do you harness that natural tendency?

Before I tell you about some of my experiences, read the following Bible passages and consider what they are really asking us to do:

> Since, then, you have been raised with Christ, set your hearts on things above, where Christ is seated at the right hand of God. Set your minds on things above, not on earthly things.[11]

To set your heart on things above is to picture (or imagine) higher things. You picture a preferred reality. Or you think about a beautiful scene that includes Jesus. To set my affection on the things of God, I need to picture Jesus having His way. To do that, I have to use my imagination.

> Let us then approach the throne of grace with confidence, so that we may receive mercy and find grace to help us in our time of need.[12]

Does God have a literal throne where He sits? Probably not. The Bible says that God is Spirit; why would a Spirit need to sit

---

11. Colossians 3:1–2
12. Hebrews 4:16

anyplace? This is metaphorical, imaginative language. God reigns supreme, and we need to come before Him as the One who holds all resources. To picture an ultimate Being sitting on a throne helps us to cement in our hearts the reality of who He is. People approaching a king on a throne are petitioning him for something that only he could grant. This imaginative language works on us in a way that straight exposition doesn't.

The Bible is giving us a picture that can help us pray. By using images, we can understand who God is, and at the same time we can use those images to help us deeply connect with Him.

For centuries, Christ-followers have been leveraging their imagination to try to grasp God's will for their lives. Saint Ignatius, from the sixteenth century, is one of the most respected mystics in the history of Christendom. And he believed and taught that using your imagination in extended times of prayer was how you could satisfy your soul. Talking words at God often doesn't satisfy. Nor does writing in a journal. Of course, I believe we need to communicate to God in those ways, but another tool in our belt needs to be harnessing our active imagination.

GOD HAS GIVEN US this ability to picture things before they happen so that they can happen. The things we fashion in the physical world begin with our fashioning them first in our mind. Every time I do a project around the house, I first picture in my mind what it will look like. I imagine what certain tiles with certain grout will look like in my bathroom. Then I set about making that vision a reality because I already know what I want. Not only does imagination help us in our planning, but when imagination becomes prayer, things happen. In fact, there are things that aren't going to happen until you pray about them.

I don't mean to sound vague. Perhaps the best way to explain what I'm talking about is to give you some specific examples from my own experience. Years ago, I—along with a group of people—imagined a church that could reach our friends who had given up on church but not on God. In our minds, we saw what a church would look like that took people's questions seriously. I could see and even hear in my mind what the music would be like. Not "cheesy-*Star-Search*-wannabe" but "loud-slammin'-raise-the-hair-on-the-back-of-your-neck get-you-God music." I could see a large, dimly lit room filled with a lot of people who were motivated to run out of the church building and be a blessing to the world. All these things have happened.

This imaginative way of praying doesn't just apply to big dreams for the future. Once I learned that a friend of mine was having marital troubles. I prayed for the couple in words and in thoughts. But then I began to pray using my imagination. I formed in my mind a picture of my friend and his wife dancing and laughing while naked—and before you think this was some sort of weird fantasy, keep reading. I figured that if he could dance and laugh naked with his wife, they would be sharing the kind of vulnerability and surrender that lead to joy. By praying that way, I was asking God to help them get to that point of vulnerability.

Their marriage is doing better today. I believe it is partially a result of God saying yes to my prayers. Choose to see God in those situations that go the way you were praying they would; don't just settle for thinking it was coincidence. Doing so will let God know that you believe in what He's doing, and it will also encourage you to pray. Because nothing motivates us to pray more than answered prayer.

THERE WAS A TIME recently when imaginative prayer got me through an extremely rough period. Some tremendously heavy things were weighing on me. I can't go into any details because the situation was so heavy and intense and of such a sensitive nature that even recounting it could cause problems. Suffice it to say, I was afraid that life as I knew it was coming to an end, and I was in a state of perpetual worry.

In times like that, I think of the truths that God has clearly, perfectly, and unconditionally communicated in the Bible. He gives this great picture of His tenderness that really spoke to my imagination at the time, and it gave me real peace:

> A bruised reed he will not break,
>   and a smoldering wick he will not snuff out.
> In faithfulness he will bring forth justice.[13]

Pondering that image during my season of brokenness, I saw myself broken and bent over but not quite snapped in two. Then I pictured God bringing His hand down and tenderly propping me up so that I wouldn't wilt or break totally in half. I imagined myself as a candle just barely smoking—almost dead, but not quite. And I saw God taking giant hands and putting them around my life so that another gust of wind wouldn't completely put out my fire. As I pictured these things, I asked God to turn those mental pictures into reality. I imagined a future that came to be.

I have never heard a voice from God, but I have received pictures from Him. I trust that God directs my imagination to form

---

13. Isaiah 42:3

pictures that are visual communiqués straight from His heart. There was a time, for instance, when I was in desperate need of God's comfort. It was a time of tension and stress, and I just needed to know that God was protecting me, sheltering me from the dangers that were all around. In my imagination, I went to a very special hiding place I had as a kid. I believe it was God who put that image in my mind.

This childhood hiding place was the hollowed-out area underneath the big evergreen tree right beside the road. I could see and hear cars whizzing by, but the people in them never knew I was there. As I went to that place in prayer, I remembered the smell of the branches, and I could feel the dirt under my rear end while my hands reached up to break a twig off of a brittle dead branch.

As I was praying, I asked Jesus to come. I saw Him crawl under the tree and sit down next to me. I'm sure my picture of Jesus wasn't accurate, but it helped me connect with Him nonetheless. I began telling Jesus my problems, and for each problem I pulled out from behind my back something that represented that particular tension point.

Before I even finished explaining the first problem, Jesus looked at me and said, "I got that." So I handed the problem over to Him. I then started explaining my second problem. He allowed me to talk because He knew it was helping me to get it all out. But just as I was finishing, He cut me off and said, "I got that."

Then I went into my third fear, which was really just a combination of the first two. This time Jesus cut me off in a curt but loving manner and said with a wave of His hand, "I got that!"

At some point in that prayer experience, I stopped actually forming the pictures and God took over. He was speaking to me, and Jesus was surprisingly curt and loving.

I said, "You're serious, aren't You?"

He said, "Yes."

Then my prayer moved from the ethereal to the physical. I began to cry. My encounter with God was so real—so visual and strong—that I was convinced God had just spoken directly to me and told me that everything was going to be okay if I would just surrender my issues to Jesus.

So don't think of prayer as a kind of speechifying. Think of prayer as something more like drawing a picture and handing it up to God, the way a kindergartner gives a picture to a parent to be posted on the refrigerator. Every parent knows that there is something precious about a piece of art created by a child who is expressing his or her wishes. Your imagination is one way to express your desires to God, and He receives that communication with joy.

> **Surrender:** putting yourself under God, doing what He wants you to do, and receiving what He has for you. This position is where you'll be closest to God, find spiritual growth, and get the most of God's power in your life.

As the Revolution takes hold in your life, be patient to learn this new way of experiencing God. Don't feel discouraged if you spend time alone with God and find it hard to harness your imagination. Don't feel bad if your imagination goes in weird directions. Don't beat yourself up if there isn't an "aha" experience. You've gotten into a relationship with God where communication has to be learned, practiced, and explored. He's not a math table to be memorized. He is a Being to be known. Patiently using all kinds of prayer techniques will help you come closer to knowing Him and seeing Him move more powerfully in and through you.

And while you pray, know this: God's Holy Spirit is praying for you.[14] The Spirit is interceding on your behalf—fighting relentlessly without pause. And that is how much you matter to God.

---

14. Romans 8:26–27

PRAYER:
LETTER FROM A REVOLUTIONARY

I always thought prayer was soft. I did it out of politeness and habit—not because I thought that it would create change. I never wanted to get my hopes up.

Two years ago, I finally owned up to the reality that abuse has unexpected effects, and one of those is disassociation. You withdraw to an inner space where you get to be alone, untouched, and terribly brave. I had found that place, and while I thought it was saving me, I realized it sucked. I withdrew from close relationships; I hated too much attention; I was nervous and unpredictable.

But finally I went to a counselor, and something bizarre happened. He asked if we could pray together. I said yes, because I was so exhausted and would try anything. As we prayed, he asked me what I was literally seeing. At that point, my mind had gone to that old place where I was completely isolated. I could see the image of a flat, skinlike, desolate field around me. Nothing was behind or ahead of me. It was useless to run. It was my recurring nightmare, and it was the worst part of my suffering.

"Bring someone else into that scene with you," the counselor said. "Ask someone you trust to come into it." And maybe you think I'd have asked for some slick angel, but I didn't. I asked God to give me my old dog. And in the middle of our prayer, in the middle of the scene of my nightmare, I suddenly felt my dog under my hand. I didn't even have to look down—he was there. Because I asked, God brought something I loved and completely trusted into a place that no one had ever been allowed to enter.

That is not soft. That is not polite prayer with no expectation. That's going back into a nightmare, recreating it, and then being saved.

CH-6

COMMUNITY

PART I: THE BIG PICTURE

I'm a heavy sleeper. I'm one of those obnoxious husbands who never hears the kids crying in the night, who asks his bleary-eyed wife in the morning, "So, how many times did the baby wake us up last night?" Once, in the middle of the night, Libby cranked the baby monitor up to eleven and stuck it in my face. The result? Continued rapid eye movement.

So when I woke up at 2:00 a.m. one December 28, I knew something was odd. And there was a strange smell throughout the house. Libby woke up to my screams of "FIRE!!!" I ran into Lena and Jake's rooms, scooping them out of their bed and crib. A friend who was recovering from a divorce and staying downstairs also heard my cries. My feet met his face at the bottom of the steps as he crawled along the floor, trying to breathe the cleaner air. For whatever reason, the smoke was no harsher than steam in my lungs.

With two kids in my arms and wearing nothing more than my underwear backward (I hope this isn't too much information for you), I sprinted over to our neighbors', my bare feet breaking through the crusty snow on the coldest night of the year.

For the next hour we watched through our neighbor's windows as the flames went from one room to the next, engulfing everything in their path. Eventually every single room and every single possession was lost either from direct contact with flames or damaged from the thick black smoke. Everything we owned was gone. All of our Christmas presents—gone. All of our clothes—gone. All of our furniture—gone. All of our pictures—gone. Everything—gone. And, by the way, we had no renter's insurance.

We stayed at Lib's parents' house for the rest of the night. The next day we ventured back over to the carnage. It was a sickening sight. Blackened aluminum siding . . . broken windows . . . our charred possessions strewn about the yard . . . our heads were swimming. On the one hand, we felt intense sadness over the loss. On the other hand, we felt intense gratitude just to be alive. The firemen told us that if we had spent thirty seconds longer in the house, we all would have died of smoke inhalation. However, He did it; God woke me up.

But we had more than that to be thankful for. Amid all that destruction, there was community. One by one our family—all of whom have been adopted into God's family—showed up to offer support. The Heintzman family had been planning to return some clothes they'd gotten for Christmas (clothes from the kind of high-end stores where we can't even afford to window-shop). Instead, they brought the unwrapped boxes to the site and said, "You need some clothes. Take these." Over the next twenty-four hours, people brought us more clothes as well as toiletries and other necessities.

One of the first people to show up was Tom Jones (not the singer). For years, he and I had been getting together every couple of weeks to talk about the deeper issues of life. We had struggled together with the things that guys struggle with. We had prayed together for power that we didn't have. On this day, we cried together.

Our dog had died in the fire. His name was Magnum, and he was a 130-pound Rottweiler. I loved that dog. If I had known he was still inside, I would have run back into the flaming house to get him. He was the first dog I had ever owned. Now I would have to bury him.

Tom Jones and other close brothers watched me bury my dog in the woods behind my backyard. They tried to help. They wanted to help. But this was something I felt I needed to do on my own. So my brothers stood by in silent support. I've cried maybe ten times in my life and probably only twice up to that point. The last time I took the Myers-Briggs assessment, I scored a zero for Feeling. I'm 100 percent Thinking. But that day, in the presence of these men, the tears flowed freely as I took a pick and shovel and started breaking through the crusty, frozen soil. The tears flowed freely because, in front of these men with whom I had been through so much, I felt the freedom to let them flow. I can still remember Jack Strobel, Andy Reamer, Chris DeFazio, John Moskal, Brian Altmeyer, and Tom Jones standing beside me as tender warriors. It felt good to bury Magnum. It felt better to have my community around me.

Jean Yanakos, one of Libby's spiritual mentors, is a person who is unusually sensitive to the leading of the Spirit. I've learned through the years that when Jean offers a word of encouragement, you'd better listen. She told us that she woke up in the middle of the night on the night of the fire, and God put a message on her heart that she didn't understand at the time: "Libby will come through the fire, but she will be spared." When she saw the story of our house fire in the next day's paper, she understood what it meant.

Jean told us that she believed our family would be like Job in the Bible—the Job who lost everything. Do you remember a couple of chapters back when I said I didn't like the story of Job? I still don't like the message that pain is unpredictable. But God gave Job back double what he lost. Jean told us that she thought we would not have to find another rental house. Instead we would own our own home and have double what we had before.

I have to admit I'm often cynical about these types of prophetic words. But as it turned out, Jean really had given us a word from the Lord. One of those guys standing with me at Magnum's burial owned a large lot that he sold us at a great price. Then God's people rallied to support us financially so we were able to make a down payment on a construction loan.

In another city, a Christ-following couple heard our story and were moved to help. They owned a furniture store, and even though they had never met us, they offered to sell us anything in the store at cost. Their church bought us an entire set of dining room furniture. Bear in mind, every place we had ever lived was decorated in "early attic" style. It was all hand-me-downs. We had never had new furniture, but now, after our "devastating" loss, we were going to have a houseful.

Your physical family is very important, but so is your spiritual family. Your spiritual family is everyone who has made the same commitment to the Revolution that you have. Your spiritual family is everyone who possesses the DNA of God. All who possess the Holy Spirit are spiritually bound together and are one.

One time Jesus was working to advance the Kingdom, and His physical family came to Him expecting Him to stop what He was doing and give them His attention. At that moment they were into their own agenda, not God's agenda. In front of everyone, Jesus said, "Here are my mother and my brothers! Whoever does God's will is my brother and sister and mother" (Mark 3:34–35). Other followers of Christ aren't *like* brothers or *similar* to sisters.

To God, they *are* brothers and sisters. Seeing this reality as a blessing and an opportunity is critical to your role in the advancement of the Revolution. So, as a result of the generosity of our brothers and sisters in Christ, Libby and I were able to buy a piece of land and build a brand-new house that was furnished with brand-new furniture. God used other people to restore our physical needs and nurture our wounded spirits. The days, weeks, and months that followed showed me that I needed my family. I needed the power of community, and that's what I got. Hillary Clinton popularized the African proverb "It takes a village to raise a child." I believe that's right. I also believe it takes a community to grow a child of God.

Our recovery from the fire wouldn't have been possible without community. Every recovery and every major advance I've ever had is partially due to the presence of other people who have a heart for God. In fact, there are very few great things God will do in your life outside of community. Most of your great moments of spiritual growth will happen around other people. Many of your "aha moments" in learning something new about God will come from other people's teaching. The times when you see the Kingdom advancing will be most powerful when you are with a group of people working on a mission.

> **Community:** people you love and who love you back—people you serve, deeply know, and celebrate . . . and people who give you all those things in return.

The Bible is all about community. Here are some examples. God Himself exists in a community of oneness: the Father, the

Son, and the Holy Spirit. God created Adam and Eve as the first human community. Abraham was called to start and lead Israel as a national community that was to bless the world. Throughout the Old Testament, teams of the nation of Israel did everything from building tabernacles and temples to fighting battles to rebuilding Jerusalem's walls and the Temple when they were destroyed. Through all these endeavors, the Kingdom grew, as did individuals in the Kingdom.

When Jesus came to Earth, He intensively cultivated community. After His cousin John baptized Him and launched His ministry, Jesus immediately set about gathering a community around Him. For the rest of His life, He not only built up people who heard Him teach and received His prayers, but He most intensively built up twelve people—His disciples. It was this community that Jesus left behind to continue the Revolution and change the world. All of God's plans were placed in the hands of twelve ordinary people who formed an extraordinary team.

Sometimes I wonder why Jesus didn't wait to come until the year 2000. (Of course, then it would be the year zero.) Couldn't He have been more powerful and effective if He came when television could beam His message around the globe? What if all His miracles could be viewed on YouTube? What if a jet could provide everyone on every continent access to see Him live or at least on a Jumbotron? And imagine how Jesus could mobilize His followers if He had e-mail!

Our technological advancements don't surprise God. He knew they were coming down the pike. So why didn't He wait to send His Son? I don't exactly know, but this I do know: what Jesus did then is the same thing He would do now—build a community and change the world.

If Jesus built a community of twelve, and if everyone in that community needed one another, then that means the world and the Kingdom need you in a community . . . and you need community. This is how the Kingdom will advance.

OFFICIAL CHURCH COMMUNITY

There are two different types of community you, as a Christ-follower, need: an official church community and an intentional friendship community.

Official church communities come in many sizes, sounds, and shapes. While some people feel very strongly about the right size, a certain music style, or a specialized theological bent, those things aren't all that important. Your church could be twelve or twelve thousand people strong, hymns or hip-hop, Calvinist or Arminian.[1] A church offers a bunch of obvious things, but the two huge elements are an authority structure and a forced agenda—in other words, an agenda that's not your agenda.

Some people find that a large organized church doesn't work for them, so they meet with people in a home environment. That's fine as long as there's an authority structure and a deliberate agenda. We all need someone who is over us, who looks out for us, and who, when appropriate, disciplines us. As you read the Bible, you will see over and over again how God sets up authorities whom we are to place ourselves under and honor. When you do that, you allow yourself to be challenged by an agenda that is not just your own.

---

1. I hate to mention theological words that aren't in the Bible, but sooner or later you are going to run into someone who uses these words as a way to identify themselves. Feel free to look into and learn from the views of camps like these, but please retain your fundamental identity as a part of the Revolution of the Kingdom.

In addition to having an agenda, each church has projects for the Kingdom they're called to take responsibility for—tangible things beyond important stuff like having worship services. Stuff like building AIDS hospices; tutoring at-risk kids; feeding people in Tanzania; reaching out to the gay community; the list goes on. No church can, nor should, do everything. But every church is called to a specific something. You need to be a part of a team that is pushing the Revolution forward in a specific niche of the world.

One friend of mine recently decided that a large, organized church wasn't for him, so he left. He said he heard from God. I don't think he did, because he left—just before a series on sex. It was the exact information with the exact kind of push that he needed to receive. By taking himself out of an organized church, he took himself away from a place where an

> **Tithing:** giving 10% of your income away to fuel the Kingdom.

agenda was being pushed on him—the very agenda that could get him outside of himself and save his heart and his marriage.

If you don't put yourself in an official church community where authorities are praying to God and planning out the future, then there are certain things that you're never going to wrestle with. I would have never chosen to learn and struggle with tithing were I not in a church that was pushing at the appropriate time and in the appropriate way. At just the right time, I've also been pushed to wrestle with things like sacrificing for my wife, considering why poverty is a major issue to God, and being challenged to amp up my prayer life. When you are doing something you shouldn't do or not doing something you should do, it's not normal to self-select a learning program in that particular area.

That is why it is critical to be with an official church community where authorities are lovingly forcing an agenda on us for the betterment of the Revolution.

Once you choose a church, it's important to stick with it. In a consumer-gets-all society, we don't really like committing. When we go out to eat, we've got a ton of options. Maybe we find a good Mexican restaurant, but if a better one opens up, we switch. And if that new restaurant doesn't do things just the way we want them, we withhold future business, speak to the manager, or leave a paltry tip.

This is classic consumerism. There's nothing inherently wrong with it, in the context of a national economy; it's the way capitalism is played, with everything from restaurants to major appliance purchases. The problems happen when we apply our consumer ways to church. A comedian summed up this consumerist attitude when he said, "Me? I'm examining the major religions. I'm looking for something that's soft on morality, generous with holidays, and has a short initiation period."

Many Bible-believing Christians shake their head in disgust at those who mix a little Buddhism with a little New Age and cover it over with a Christian veneer. Some of those same "theologically correct" people, however, do something very similar by mixing Christianity with American consumerism and refusing to commit to a church they can pour their lives into. It fits well with our consumerist spirituality to dabble in about three churches—one with the traditional trappings to make us feel legitimate, another with great music and teaching, and then a third that provides other solid programs. We want a "perfect" church experience.

The problem is, this kind of consumerism is inherently anti-community. Why? Because even if you are a good consumer, all you're doing is consuming. Community thrives in the give and take. Community can't happen without a commitment to love, serve, know, and celebrate one another.

> Let us hold unswervingly to the hope we profess, for he who promised is faithful. And let us consider how we may spur one another on toward love and good deeds. Let us not give up meeting together, as some are in the habit of doing, but let us encourage one another—and all the more as you see the Day approaching.[2]

You won't find the phrase "church membership" anywhere in the Bible. But the principles for church membership are everywhere, including this passage. The only way to "spur one another on" is to meet regularly with the same people.

Yet there's a limit to the depth of community that any church can provide. And being a church attendee doesn't mean you are automatically part of a healthy community, because community isn't about just showing up for a specified period of time. Community is also about fulfilling the specific functions that God calls Christ-followers to fulfill as a team. A community that is working the way it ought to work is a powerful thing. Check out this picture of the local church community in Jerusalem in the first century AD:

> They devoted themselves to the apostles' teaching and to the fellowship, to the breaking of bread and to prayer. Everyone was filled with awe, and many wonders and miraculous signs were done by the apostles. All the believers were together and had everything in common. Selling their possessions and goods,

---

2. Hebrews 10:23–25

WELCOME TO THE REVOLUTION

they gave to anyone as he had need. Every day they continued to meet together in the temple courts. They broke bread in their homes and ate together with glad and sincere hearts, praising God and enjoying the favor of all the people. And the Lord added to their number daily those who were being saved.[3]

Among other things, the marks of healthy community are found in this passage:

- A devotion to teaching the Bible
- A belief in the power of prayer
- A commitment to doing life together
- Working a mission that resulted in a good reputation in the community at large and numerical growth

As a new Christ-follower, you've probably never taken church membership seriously and actually shopped around for a church. Ouch! I just used a consumerist word in relation to choosing a church—the very thing I said not to do. Nevertheless, I'm going to keep that image of shopping because it's okay—even neces-sary—to "shop" for a church once, as long as you're doing it with an eye toward commitment. That's a different thing from renting a church on a week-by-week basis the way you rent a table at a res-taurant on a meal-by-meal basis. You need to keep your options open, but only so you can make a commitment. Looking over the menu is great, but at some point you've got to put away the menu and eat your meal.

So let's return to those marks of a healthy church community so you have some criteria to use when you're shopping:

---

3. Acts 2:42–47

A HEALTHY CHURCH COMMUNITY DEVOTES ITSELF TO TEACHING THE BIBLE.

The first-century church in Jerusalem "devoted themselves to the apostles' teaching." (The apostles were the guys who wrote the New Testament.) A healthy church teaches the Bible as the supreme authority.

If you go to a church that doesn't refer to the Bible or if the Bible is used merely in keeping with the day's liturgy or to justify current behavior, beware! Not only will it not be possible for you to grow spiritually in a church that doesn't believe in God's Word, but that church will lack the power of God. Churches that don't teach the Bible really don't believe the Bible. If you don't believe the Bible, you aren't doing what God says to do. And if you aren't doing what God says to do, God isn't honored—and He isn't involved.

A HEALTHY CHURCH COMMUNITY BELIEVES IN THE POWER OF PRAYER.

The Christ-followers in Jerusalem devoted themselves to prayer because they believed in its power. It was through prayer that miracles happened. As the apostles prayed, they were able to do "miraculous signs and wonders."

I must admit that I've rarely seen things that I would describe as "signs and wonders." When I think of a wonder, I think of cancer being healed or a blind person gaining sight without medical intervention. I wish the churches I've been involved with saw more of those kinds of signs and wonders. However, I know that the churches I've been involved with believed that God could and would do wonderful things if they prayed. When my friend's newborn was diagnosed with a heart problem, we prayed, believing that God could heal him and that there would be no need for open-heart surgery. To date, he hasn't needed it. If we don't believe in the power of prayer and then pray for big things with bold expectancy, we really don't believe.

One more thing. Answered prayers aren't mere coincidences. Claim everything positive as God's work.

Not believing in the power of prayer is inextricably linked with not believing in the power of God. The only people who have a hard time with the power of God are those who have never truly experienced God's power through a great relationship with Him.

A HEALTHY CHURCH COMMUNITY DOES LIFE WITH ONE ANOTHER.

People who are part of healthy churches do life with one another; they "have everything in common," as the writer of Acts described it. I'm not talking about communal living; I'm talking about a holistic approach involving community in every area of life, not just Sunday mornings. That kind of connection makes the church healthy and, in turn, makes the members spiritually healthy.

After the fire, why did my friends give my family their clothes instead of returning them and getting money for themselves? Because they believe that their stuff isn't actually their stuff. They believe that everything is God's stuff: He places it on loan with individuals who are to share it with others in the community. That assignment includes "giving to everyone as he had need."

But doing life with one another means more than helping out in the midst of pain. It also means worshipping together as the Jerusalem church did, meeting "together in the temple courts," and then laughing with one another while dining together "with glad and sincere hearts." It takes more than great teaching and great programs to make a great church. A great church fosters real-life community; a great church encourages people to do life together.

A HEALTHY CHURCH COMMUNITY HAS A GOOD REPUTATION IN THE COMMUNITY AT LARGE.

A healthy church enjoys "the favor of all the people," which means that in the town or city where the church is located, even those who aren't followers of Christ think highly of both the church and those who go there. Of course there will be times when a church teaches things that bring disdain from those who aren't following Jesus. There are plenty of truths in the Bible that aren't popular in the world at large. In our "live and let live" society, people who take a stand for truth will often be seen in unfavorable terms.

Unfortunately, though, local churches rarely earn disdain because of what they teach. Instead, they earn disdain for what they do or what they leave undone. Too many waitresses have seen the after-church crowd bow their heads in generous prayers of thanks and then leave miserable tips. Too few churches get involved in the social ills of their city. They sit back and give pious reasons for why the ills exist, but rarely do they get in the mud to fix the problem. Too many families in the church are just regular old dysfunctional families with a religious veneer. Too many churches fight and compete with one another over which one is truly biblical or which is the best place to give your money. Too many churches strive to be just like everyone else in hopes of not offending, and in the process they end up not looking much like the family of God.

All of this adds up to a church that doesn't have a good reputation in the community. Unbelievers should see members of Christian communities loving one another and living life in such a way as to inspire them to seek Christ. Jesus said, "By this all men will know that you are my disciples, if you love one another."[4] Notice that Jesus didn't say, "All men will know that you are My disciples if you are cheap, isolationist, dysfunctional, selfish, and judgmental."

So, if you can, find a church whose departure from the city

---

4. John 13:35

would prompt the citizens to say, "We're screwed without them." If that church doesn't exist, then work to make the church you're involved with become that kind of church community. Or, consider that God may be asking you to be part of a team that starts a brand new church. Can you imagine what would happen in churches and in our society if all of us lived lives transformed by the power of a Kingdom-driven community?

A HEALTHY CHURCH COMMUNITY GROWS NUMERICALLY.

It's natural for healthy things to grow. Every organism that is healthy reproduces itself and adds to its number. Likewise, a healthy church is a community that grows. The early church wasn't making itself grow by tapping into market-share techniques. Rather, "the Lord added to their number daily those who were being saved." God chose to add people to the Jerusalem community because He saw it as a place where infant followers could be taught the Bible, pray with one another, do life with one another, and, as a community, make a statement to everyone in the area that God was Someone special who was doing something awesome in their midst.

I don't care if you're a Myers-Briggs capital-I Introvert who scored a zero on extroversion. You are not dismissed from the responsibility and ensuing blessing of getting outside of yourself and getting inside a community. This is not a responsibility placed on your shoulders as a burden to bear. This is an opportunity placed on your shoulders so that you will be able to bear the burden of life.

INTENTIONAL FRIENDSHIP COMMUNITIES

Now for the friendship communities. One sign that people are taking control of their own lives is that they're also taking control of their friendships. Healthy friendships rarely just happen. Just as you are what you eat (I'm a combo of bananas, cheese combos, and wings, myself), you are who you spend time with. We understandably try to make very strategic decisions when it comes to career choices, major purchases, and workout plans. These things all matter to God, but not more than the people we spend time with. Creating an intentional friendship community will grow you beyond your individual ability, and it will give you a safety net when life's hard knocks get you down.

In college, I lived in a big house with a bunch of guys. It wasn't a frat house, but it was off-campus and consisted entirely of virile young men seeking God. This didn't mean we studied the Bible every day after waking up to "Kum-Ba-Yah." A few more Bible studies probably would have been a good idea, but "Kum-Ba-Yah" is never good for anyone with a testosterone count.

One of the things we did do was catch arrows. We had found an old door and a bow with a few arrows . . . not a good combination for virile young men and no moms. So two guys would go out into the yard, each holding an end of the door, while someone else would shoot an arrow high into the air. The arrow would speed straight toward the atmosphere, finally slow to a stop, and then start to fall. Eventually the arrow would flip with the pointed end hurtling straight back toward Earth. The object of the game was to catch the arrow with the wooden door. (Thankfully, that was the only wood we ever hit.) Good times. Stupid, maybe, but fun. We laughed together, we learned together, we prayed together, and we struggled together. We made intentional choices to be around each other and spur one another to growth.

The Bible says to "not forsake the assembling together, as is the habit of some, but to meet with one another and encourage one another" (Hebrews 10:23–25). For the Revolution inside of you to go forward you must intentionally find a group of friends who want to find God in deeper ways. Then you must intentionally structure time with those people so that you can grow with one another, support one another, and laugh with one another. This is what is often called a "small group." They don't accidentally happen. They intentionally happen.

That great theologian Rocky Balboa understood something about how community works when he talked about his relationship with Adrian: "I've got gaps; she's got gaps. Together, we've got no gaps." This is what happens with a friendship community. It enables us to grow, fill in, heal, and change.

An intentional friendship community is what ministered to my family during our time of need after the fire and allowed us to get back double of what we had lost. Just as Jean had said to Libby, we got through the fire, and we were spared. Two years after I buried Magnum with my friends circled around me, we got a new Rottweiler. We named him Job.

PART II: EXAMINE YOUR INDIVIDUAL RELATIONSHIPS

Now that we've talked about the big picture of community—plugging into a church where you can contribute and receive support and help and joy—let's move on to understanding the one-on-one relationships and the role these play in the big picture of your life. Because, ultimately, this is how you advance the Revolution: one-on-one.

We can't be spiritually healthy if we aren't relationally healthy. We've looked at methods for Bible reading and methods for prayer, so now I'd like to look at a method for monitoring your personal relationships. What does it mean to be relationally healthy? It means that we monitor our relational meter, and we recognize what various people do to the needle on that meter. Relationships are like the buttons on an elevator. They will either take you up or take you down. Every personal interaction you have will leave you with a little more energy for your day or a little less, and these energy fluctuations affect your spiritual vitality.

In my early years of following Jesus, I read a book that has shaped my relational life ever since: Gordon MacDonald's *Restoring Your Spiritual Passion*. It sensitized me to the fact that those who are around me will either make me or break me, and they will also set the pace for my spiritual development.

I'll sum up Gordon's thesis on one-on-one relationships by saying that every person in your life can be categorized according to whether they increase your energy and passion or sap your energy and passion.

Before we go further, let me clarify something: everybody is a VIP (Very Important Person) in God's eyes. However, the people in your life will all have a different effect on you. You have to account for that when you consider how you're going to spend your time relationally. To put it another way, you need to use discretion. Discretion helps you to execute a plan and put in place a system that will enable you to be healthy.

Discretion will protect you,
    and understanding will guard you.
Wisdom will save you from the ways of wicked men,
    from men whose words are perverse.[5]

---

5. Proverbs 2:11–12

I've shared this system with a lot of people, and I want to eliminate two common misconceptions right up front. First, this is not justification for never spending time with people who aren't Christians. True, people who aren't trying to follow Christ can have a negative impact on your growth. But the truth is, anybody can have a negative impact on your growth—even some preachers. These five categories are to be applied to individuals you are in relationship with, not to whole groups of people. You can't say that all nonbelievers or all French people or all circus clowns are VDPs (Very Draining Persons) who are strictly to be avoided.

A second but related misconception is that categorizing people is somehow sinful. Categorizing a person you don't know—that's sinful. That's called bigotry. I'm encouraging you to be discerning about people after you've gotten to know them. Now, on to the categories.

Category	Relational Charge	Comments
Very Energizing Person (VEP)	+++ (Triple Positive)	VEPs build your passion
Very Similar Person (VSP)	++ (Double Positive)	VSPs share your passion
Very Teachable Person (VTP)	+ (Positive)	VTPs receive your passion
Very Nice Person (VNP)	Neutral	VNPs enjoy your passion
Very Draining Person (VDP)	- (Negative)	VDPs drain your passion

VERY ENERGIZING PEOPLE BUILD OUR PASSION (+++).

Very Energizing People (VEPs) build into our lives. They cause us to advance. Think about the people about whom you would say, "If it weren't for him, I don't know where I would be today" or "She taught me everything I know." Those people are VEPs in your life.

Jesus was a VEP for the people who knew Him. People knew He was going to build into them when they were around Him. One minute He was making them laugh; the next minute He was feeding them. One minute He was encouraging them; the next minute He was teaching them. One minute He was hugging on them; the next minute He was offering them a word to grow on. One minute He was grieving with them; the next minute He was healing them. When people came away from being with Jesus, they were far better off than before their interaction. As a result, a lot of people wanted Jesus' time. People are drawn to people who fuel their spiritual passion.

When you come away from being with a VEP, you hold your head a little higher, you have fresh thoughts, and you feel better about yourself. You may have been questioned and challenged. When you are done with these people, you are at a new level. One example of a VEP in my life is my father-in-law, Roger Neubauer. I come away from him being encouraged and built up. He doesn't have a perfect life, but he does have a life I can learn and grow from. As a matter of fact, when I finished the first chapter of this book and realized I was in over my head, Roger was the first person I called for help and constructive criticism.

My wife also energizes me to an unbelievable level—not just because she builds into me spiritually and emotionally, but because she does so physically too. Tuesday nights are garbage nights on our street. Last Tuesday night I came home exhausted at 11:00, dreading that I still had to mess with the garbage before I could fall into bed. But when my headlights swung into the driveway, I saw that the garbage was out. It wasn't Libby's job to take care of the garbage. Nobody would have faulted her if she had left it for me to do, but she chose to serve me. She was thinking of me, knowing that I would be coming in late. That kind of stuff charges me up and enhances our relationship. Find VEPs and get as many of them in your life as you possibly can.

People were bummed when it was time for Jesus to leave them. No one wants to see a VEP leave. When Jesus had to leave, He told His friends that they would get the Holy Spirit. They would then have an intimate and internal relationship with God. Here, recorded in the Bible, is what He said on the subject:

> But I tell you the truth: It is for your good that I am going away. Unless I go away, the Counselor will not come to you; but if I go, I will send him to you.[6]

The Holy Spirit (the Counselor) is not a force but a Person—a Very Energizing Person. All Christ-followers have a built-in VEP who has been personally dispatched by Jesus. It is important to look for people who have the same internal Counselor and who can have an energizing influence on your spiritual development. By the same token, it is important that you be a VEP for the people in your life. After all, you have the power source of the Holy Spirit within you.

VERY SIMILAR PEOPLE SHARE OUR PASSION (++).

Very Similar People (VSPs) are those who are in sync with your values. For whatever reason, things just click when you are together. It could be because you view the world similarly. It could be because

---

6. John 16:7

you have a similar temperament. It could be because you have a passion for the same things, share a similar sense of humor, or have the same hobbies.

More specifically, the VSPs I'm talking about here are those who are on the same path in the pursuit of Christlikeness that you are. One minute a VSP is building your spirit, and in the very next minute you are building his or hers.

Because Jesus was the Son of God, it's hard to imagine Him finding a VSP, but He did. He had a friend (his cousin, as a matter of fact) called John the Baptist. John was a godly man who understood the concepts of sacrifice, commitment, and the value of giving his life wholly to God. One day, John's friends came to him and were a bit upset. The story they told him went something like this: "Hey, more and more of the crowd is following Jesus. We are losing our base of followers. This has to stop."

John answered, basically, that he was cool with that: "That joy is mine, and it is now complete. He must become greater; I must become less."[7]

I think Jesus must have gotten a positive charge from John. John understood who Jesus was, the unique demands of His life, and Jesus' need for support. VSPs have that special ability to understand what we may not even understand about ourselves. VSPs give us a double-plus charge compared to the average person. Maybe it is because these relationships are so low maintenance. Maybe it is because you don't have to explain yourself as often because the other person intuitively understands what you are about. Maybe it is because they offer counsel that is razor sharp and accurate. But it is definitely because they share your passion for growing in intimacy with Christ. You can never have too many VSPs.

---

7. John 3:29–30

VERY TEACHABLE PEOPLE RECEIVE OUR PASSION (+).

What is teachability? It's simply a person's propensity for growth.
The only limitation to a person's teachability is his or her personal
desire. Not everyone will grow at the same rate if taught the same
information, but everyone can be taught. The more teachable you
are, the more of a joy you are to be around.

Look at what the Bible says about the qualifications of a leader
in the local church:

> A servant of the Lord must not argue. Instead, he must be kind
> to everyone, *teachable*, willing to suffer wrong.[8]

Translators go back and forth over whether or not this word
should be translated from Greek as "able to teach" or "teachable."
As a pastor, I can tell you that there are a lot of people who are good
leaders yet can't teach in a way that holds your attention, but I don't
know anybody who is a good leader and can't be taught. The worst
leaders are arrogant and boastful. Prideful people can't be taught
because they believe that what they already possess is better than
what someone else can give them.

Very Teachable People (VTPs) are people who grow as a result
of your energy. They learn and advance in life. Sometimes these
relationships don't give you an immediate charge because they
take some effort. But, on the whole, it is energizing to see your life
having an impact on others.

If someone is getting a constant score of 90 percent in life,
but they aren't growing, I don't get too much energy from that
person. On the other hand, a person who is only indexing at 48
percent this month—but last month he was at 47 and the month

---

8. 2 Timothy 2:24, italics mine, paraphrased

before that he was at 46—that person gives me energy. There is something special about people who are growing.

So I make sure that I have people in my life to whom I can offer things, and then I arrange my schedule accordingly. Right now I have a small group of strong men who are new to following Christ. We meet every Monday at 6:30 a.m. I'm inspired every time I come away from these times of community. I learn from these guys, and when they learn from me, my energy meter ticks north.

Right now you are probably in a position of teachability in your relationship to Christ-followers who are more mature than you. You need to ask yourself how teachable you really are. Are you willing to admit that your views of heaven and hell were misinformed? Are you willing to admit that you are selfish and need God's help? Are you willing to admit that you need to reexamine your sexual practices in light of God's Word?

You may feel you don't have much to bring to the community of Christ-followers. You may feel you're in the position only of receiving, not giving. But just being teachable and growing does more to energize the Christ-followers around you than you know.

For instance, I've got a friend named David. This guy had no church background or Bible knowledge before he started hanging around our church, but that didn't mean he didn't have anything to teach us. He shared a story with me that was deeply energizing.

David is a headhunter: he matches potential high-level execs with private and public companies. When one of David's business owner clients is in the final step of the hiring process, he'll ask the candidate if they can swing by the grocery store on the way back to the airport. As they go through the aisles, the candidate wheels the cart while the owner loads up on groceries and makes small talk. The owner pays, loads the groceries into the trunk, and walks back around the car while he keeps making small talk. Finally, the owner gets into the car and looks into the rearview mirror to see what the candidate does.

No matter how impressive the education, credentials, track record or interview has been, if the candidate doesn't take the cart back to the designated area in the parking lot, *he is not hired.* The cart doesn't belong wedged between two cars or even in an empty parking space. It belongs in the designated area. Integrity demands it.

The owner figures if the candidate won't exhibit a work ethic and take the path of integrity on something as simple as returning a cart, there's no way the owner can trust the candidate in other more significant matters.

By sharing this story, David gave me fresh insight into integrity and how God is always watching and noticing our diligence. David and I are both being VTPs: I'm helping him learn what it means to follow Jesus, and he's teaching me new ways to understand diligence.

(By the way . . . you are now "cursed." Never again will you be able to take the slacker route with the cart. I'm guessing that for the rest of your life you'll do the right thing in this area or live with the consequences of being a loser!)

VERY NICE PEOPLE ENJOY OUR PASSION.

Do you remember that old Warner Brothers cartoon with the two dogs? I think they were called Myron and Spike. Myron was the little yappy varmint. Then there was his friend, Spike, the big bulldog with the spiked collar. Spike went about his business, and Myron was always jumping back and forth over the top of him saying in a high-pitched yappy squeal, "Hey, Spike! How are you doing, Spike? How are you, Spike? Where are you going, Spike?" Myron was very nice. He wasn't bringing Spike down, but he wasn't energizing him either.

This is what happens with nice people. Very Nice People (VNPs) enjoy our passion and always hang around, but they don't energize us. Now there's nothing wrong with nice people, but Jesus didn't live and die to make nice people out of us.

> **God's Word / Word of God:** the Bible; God's heart and instructions captured on paper.

When Jesus went into Jerusalem for the last time, the streets were crowded with nice people. They found Jesus interesting. They appreciated His passion. They waved palm branches and sang, "Hosanna," and said all sorts of nice things. But less than a week later, many of the same people were part of a mob, screaming, "Kill Him. Kill Him!"

There will never be a shortage of nice people. Nice people are often nice because they're faking it. And that's draining. No one likes a faker. Think about professional wrestling: in the past, the folks involved were always afraid of what would happen if they were proven to be fake (even though we all knew it). Interestingly enough, when professional wrestling publicly admitted that it was a show and not authentic, its revenues soared. There's tremendous power in being real, even when that reality isn't pretty.

Churches are filled with VNPs who aren't able to be anything other than nice because they refuse to be real with one another. When people aren't sharing their nasties, how are they going to get encouragement? When folks aren't sharing their weaknesses, how are they going to get support? VNPs often subtly compete with one another for who has a cleaner life. Then, when someone messes up, they pounce. Very Nice People and Very

Nice Communities are neutral to our spiritual growth in their best times and negative in their worst times. Tread carefully and lightly around these types.

VERY DRAINING PEOPLE SAP OUR PASSION (−).

Very Draining People (VDPs) come in various shapes and sizes. VDPs sap our passion and have a negative effect on us. There are "One-Minus" people and there are "Triple-Minus" people who suck you dry like a wet/dry Shop-Vac. VDPs will drain different people to varying degrees. Some people who are VDPs to you are VNPs or even VSPs to other people. I have friends who get a charge out of certain people who drain me. And there are people who energize me but would suck the life out of some of you. The important thing is to realize when someone has a draining effect on you, and then make the necessary modifications.

What kind of modifications? Sometimes it's as simple as not answering the phone when you see a VDP's name on your caller ID. That's not to say you need to cut every needy person out of your life, but you do need to be aware of your own levels of relational energy. If you're in the black relationally—thanks to the energizing people in your life—maybe you've got adequate surplus to pick up the phone and have a conversation with a VDP. If you're already drained, there's nothing wrong with letting the phone ring and calling back when the time's better for you.

When the crowds were getting to Him, Jesus would go off by Himself, or He would go with His disciples, specifically the ones who had a positive effect on His energy. Among the twelve disciples, Peter, James, and John seem to have gotten more of Jesus' time. John came to be called "the beloved." Was that because Jesus got a positive charge from him? Maybe so. Whatever the case, Jesus spent a lot of time with John.

Jesus also told His followers that they needed to be aware of how people were affecting them as they did ministry. When He sent His followers into the neighborhoods to speak about God's truth, Jesus gave them these instructions:

> If the home is deserving, let your peace rest on it; if it is not, let your peace return to you. If anyone will not welcome you or listen to your words, shake the dust off your feet when you leave that home or town.[9]

Jesus was saying: "If you try to build into people and offer them your peace and joy but they do nothing with it, move on. Forget about that relationship. Your run is done, and you aren't held responsible." I have seen person after person who had a fire for God yet the Revolution went down in flames. It's often because they didn't understand how to monitor their relational levels. I also know person after person who is living a substandard life because, relationally, they haven't got it nailed down.

Remember that everything affects everything else. You cannot be spiritually healthy if you are not relationally healthy.

ARE YOU A VDP?

I suspect this talk about VEPs, VNPs and VDPs really, really grates on some of you. Could it be because you don't want to admit that you are a drain on people around you? It is possible that you are a VDP. Oww! Oww! If you can at least recognize that, you are showing signs of teachability. The sooner you recognize your effect on others, accept that reality, and then start to grow, the better off your life and your relationship with God will be.

Here are some questions for you to consider. If you answer yes to two or more of these questions, you might be a VDP:

---

9. Matthew 10:13–14

- Do people regularly abandon me as a friend?
- Do I find that people quite often don't return my phone calls promptly—or don't return them at all?
- Do I speak more than I listen?
- Do my conversations tend to drift toward what is wrong with the world, life, and other people?
- Do I consider conversations "wasted" unless my agenda or I myself am the main topic of the conversation?
- Is it rare for me to laugh in my conversations with people?

Many spiritually draining Christians are that way because they have never had the blessing of community. They have never been in a safe place where somebody was willing and able to deliver an uncomfortable message in a very tender way. There is hope for you if you sense you are a VDP. Why? Because you have the Holy Spirit, the ultimate VEP, living inside you.

HOW TO STAY RELATIONALLY HEALTHY

Relational health doesn't just happen. You have to be intentional. Here are some strategies for making sure your relationships are helping you grow into the person God wants you to be.

ASSESS YOUR RELATIONSHIPS.

He who walks with the wise grows wise,
    but a companion of fools suffers harm.[10]

Assessing your relationships is different from classifying your

---

10. Proverbs 13:20

relationships. Classifying carries with it the assumption that something has always been a particular way and always will be. You should not limit a person's potential or the potential of a relationship. But you should take stock of the effect that people have on you and make the necessary accommodations, even if that means moving them out of your life.

ADJUST YOUR RATIOS.

It is not enough to just have some people in the positive-charge categories. We have to have a preponderance of VEPs, VSPs, and VTPs versus VDPs in our lives. Think about a committee you serve on or a team at work. If just one person out of eight has a negative drain, everybody feels it, but you can probably overcome it. You need a 12:1 ratio of positive energy to negative energy. Jesus' VDP was Judas. If Jesus needed eleven people to offset his VDP, we need at least that many.

> "Be careful," Jesus said to them. "Be on your guard against the yeast of the Pharisees and Sadducees."[11]

Yeast is something that is of very small mass, but it affects and infects the entire batch of dough. Likewise, it only takes a little time for VDPs to negatively affect your life. You should spend time with VDPs. After all, they matter to God. But at the same time, you have to be aware of the impact they will have on your vitality.

AMPLIFY YOUR ENERGY.

Become a VEP for the people in your life. What are you doing to become an energizing person? Hopefully, once you understand the truths found in this book, you will advance significantly in

---

11. Matthew 16:6

your walk with Jesus, which will naturally make you an energizing person to be around. People loved being around Jesus. People love being around people who are like Jesus, who have had Jesus formed inside of them.

COMMUNITY:
LETTER FROM A REVOLUTIONARY

NEW BELIEVER AND MATURE BELIEVER, URBAN AND SUBURBAN, TATTOOS AND PEARLS. AT FIRST, NO ONE WOULD HAVE PUT US TOGETHER. THE ONLY COMMONALITY THAT INITIALLY LINKED THE PEOPLE WITH WHOM I NOW SHARE THE MOST INTIMATE DETAILS OF MY LIFE—HIGHS AND LOWS, CRISES AND CELEBRATIONS—WAS A SHARED DESIRE TO LIVE INTENTIONALLY, CONNECTED TO A COMMUNITY IN A DEEPER AND MORE INTIMATE WAY THAN THE CASUAL ACQUAINTANCES AND DRINKING-BUDDY FRIENDSHIPS WE'D EXPERIENCED IN THE PAST.

SO ON A SEEMINGLY RANDOM TUESDAY MORNING, I HELD MY BREATH AND SENT A STRANGE E-MAIL TO NEARLY COMPLETE STRANGERS.

ONE BY ONE, RESPONSES CAME BACK, AND OUR FLEDGLING COALITION OF WOULD-BE COMMUNITY-LIVERS BEGAN TO FORM. WE FLOUNDERED FOR AT LEAST A YEAR BEFORE HITTING ON WHAT WE WERE REALLY TRYING TO DO: TO SHARE THE ENTIRETY OF OUR LIVES TOGETHER, PRETTY OR NOT—AND

ESPECIALLY NOT. SINCE THEN, WE'VE CELEBRATED BIRTHS AND MOURNED THE LOSS OF CHILDREN. WE'VE BAPTIZED ONE ANOTHER AND FOUGHT FOR EACH OTHER'S MARRIAGES. WE'VE THROWN BLOWOUT PARTIES AND PULLED TOGETHER WHATEVER CASH WE COULD FIND TO PAY ONE ANOTHER'S DEBTS. AND WE'VE FUMBLED THROUGH ALL OF THIS IN HOPES OF KNOWING JESUS MORE AND RECEIVING HIS TRUTH AND LOVE FOR US IN THE MIDST OF COMMUNITY.

MISSION

What does it look like when God gets hold of your life? You get hold of the world. You become a giant love machine. You become a man or a woman on a mission.

There's a conflict going on around us, all the time, on every square inch of this Earth. And God hasn't called us to live like we're on vacation in the middle of this warring land—He's called us to live the Kingdom right here. He's asked us take on the sinful ways of the world and love the hell out of it (pun intended). To ignore that call to action is to miss an incredible opportunity.

When you see friends killing themselves on a path of addiction, what do you do? You jump in with love. You jump in and speak straight truth and help them get out of it. When you see someone who has financial hardship, what do you do? Write a check. It's God's money. You see a guy with a flat tire as you're pulling out of your office parking lot? You ignore the urge to get home and again crash in front of the TV, and you pull over and change his tire because you want to serve him.

There's an old line that people don't care how much you know until they know how much you care. Long gone are the days of intense analytical discussion of what it means to believe the Bible and get Jesus. Don't get me wrong. A lot of people need intricate rationale for the existence of God and the supremacy of Jesus, and we can't check our brains at the church door. But most people want to simply see how it works. We want to see action, because action is what we believe.

Look how Jesus did it: He invited people to follow Him. He ate dinner with them. He pulled them off the street when they were in pain. He got quiet and sat down with them when they needed a good listener. Jesus blessed the world. We are called to do the same: bless people no matter where we are, no matter where we're going, no matter what day it is.

Prayer, the Bible, and community exist to support the mission of the Kingdom of God. Those are extremely important support systems. But the Kingdom's purpose—our mission—is to make this world operate according to love. That's the way God intends us to live.

Other than the Bible, the world's best-selling book is *The Purpose-Driven Life* by Rick Warren. More people have bought that book, by far, than any other book in history. Why? Because all of us want to know our purpose, our mission. Sometimes when I'm speaking to large groups, I ask if they've read *The Purpose-Driven Life*. As many as 90 percent say yes. Then my next question is, "What's your purpose?" I get a lot of shrugs.

People think they have to polish up their mission and do it Bono-style or Mother Teresa-style. They think they need to end world poverty, fix the American education system, get the Bengals to the Super Bowl. But in the end, very few of us will knock out these huge things. What we are going to knock out is the day-by-day loving.

You've got to start; you've got to move. The best car to steer is the one that's moving. If you wait to have the perfect mission, the perfect purpose, you won't go anywhere. Instead, look around. Look down your street. Look at the next cube over. Look at the kids at the bus stop. And then stand up and push the Kingdom forward. In the process, your relationship with God and your understanding of His desires will be pushed forward.

I know two hundred people who are pushing the Kingdom forward—two hundred adults in Cincinnati who are tutoring high-risk elementary kids. These are kids with little hope, kids who don't get looked after very much. In the history of their school, none of the administrators can remember any child going on to college. None. So what did these two hundred people do? They said no to that educational inequity. They said no to a lack of adult and parental involvement in the lives of these kids, and they got down and pushed the Kingdom.

You know what's happening to those kids? Their test scores are going crazy. In math, they're up 55 percent. In reading, 25 percent. And while those kids are expanding their minds, the two hundred adults are learning what it means to be revolutionary and change things life-by-life, hour-by-hour. Sounds strikingly close to what Jesus does, right? He gets down with us—to a child's level—and shows us love. I'll tell you something else: when you are involved with something like that, it's easier to read the Bible, pray big prayers, and foster community.

A BIG QUESTION YOU'RE going to be asking yourself as you pray, listen to others, and think through this new way of life is *How do I know if I'm hearing the right mission? Am I supposed to go to South*

Africa? Am I supposed to just be quiet and give grace to my friend when she's reaming me out?

Here's a simple test: any thought or idea you have that you think Jesus would like that's the thing to do. So do it. That's your mission. And if you hear something you don't like hearing, but you're still hearing it, and you know it's making Jesus smile? Yeah. That is definitely your mission.

Never pray for something you aren't willing to be the answer for. If you have the heart for something, it's probably your mission. If you're praying about it, work on it. You are very likely to be the answer to the prayers you pray. That doesn't mean God is not involved. He is actually working through you. You're His hands, His feet, His eyes.

God didn't say, "Hey, Adam and Eve, get your gardening plan together and then come back and run it by Me so I can make sure it's perfect." Not at all. And He didn't tell Adam to go to Him for final approval of all the names he gave the animals. (Otherwise He might have rejected "aardvark.") God commissioned Adam and Eve, and God trusted them. God has commissioned you, and God is trusting you.

THE BIBLE SOMETIMES REFERS to the people of God as "the body of Christ"; each of us is a different body part, so to speak. We each have a different function (just as an eye has a different function from an elbow), but together we act as a unified body. What do a Revolution and a body have in common? Both of them are in constant motion when they're healthy.

I've had a broken finger, two broken arms, and countless

stitches. The worst stitches came after I chose to take out the garbage in bare feet. Libby must have accidentally dropped my empty bottle next to the trash can. I didn't see the broken bottle before my foot came down on top of it with 180 pounds of pressure. I severed tendons and hobbled around for weeks. When you get injured, the pain of the moment is bad, but even worse is the immobilization that follows. Our bodies are meant to go places. When part of your body is unhealthy or broken, it affects your ability to move forward.

In the same way, when you—a member of the body of Christ—aren't spiritually healthy, or when you don't understand what your role is, or when you choose not to fulfill it, the Revolution of the Kingdom of God suffers. Consider how God describes this situation:

> Now the body is not made up of one part but of many. If the foot should say, "Because I am not a hand, I do not belong to the body," it would not for that reason cease to be part of the body. And if the ear should say, "Because I am not an eye, I do not belong to the body," it would not for that reason cease to be part of the body. If the whole body were an eye, where would the sense of hearing be? If the whole body were an ear, where would the sense of smell be? But in fact God has arranged the parts in the body, every one of them, just as he wanted them to be. If they were all one part, where would the body be? As it is, there are many parts, but one body.
>
> The eye cannot say to the hand, "I don't need you!" And the head cannot say to the feet, "I don't need you!" . . . If one part suffers, every part suffers with it; if one part is honored, every part rejoices with it.

Now you are the body of Christ, and each one of you is a
part of it.[1]

You have value in the progress of the Kingdom. You say you're
only a toe? Many an NFL career has ended because of a toe that
wouldn't heal. Maybe you're a brain, but if you choose to think
only about things that bring you money, sex, and power, then God
won't do through you all the things He wants to do.

I know Christ-followers who know the Bible, pray regularly,
and enjoy community but don't have a compelling sense of mission. Your mission is the task that God has equipped you for that
no one else can do. No one else can show your boss that being a
Christ-follower leads you to love more and maybe work harder
as you honor her authority. If you have a spouse, no one else can
love that person like you can. If you fail to love your spouse, not
only will your household suffer, but your faith and the Revolution
will suffer too. If you have kids, you are the person to raise them
to know the Lord. If you don't do so, then not only will they not
grow spiritually, but the Kingdom will suffer because its future
warriors aren't being trained.

Something magical happens when gifted people bring their
energy to fields of engagement that God cares about. And what fields
does God care about? All of them. God cares about your school.
Your neighborhood? That too. Where you work? Absolutely. Those
are all places where the Kingdom seeks to take new territory.

Every realm of your world should operate according to the
heart of God—a heart that is full of love and health. Wherever
there is hate, pride, ineffectiveness, and frustration, it is because
God isn't having His way. He gets His way—a way of love, humility,

1. 1 Corinthians 12:14–21, 26–27

effectiveness, and success—when warriors in the Kingdom do their jobs.

ONE OF THE TRITE phrases that exists in churches (and on bumpers) is "Let go and let God." It's absolutely true that God has a power that we don't possess and that He can do things that we will never be able to do. When we allow Him to work and when we yield to His power, great things happen. However, it is also true that, more times than not, God uses His people to get Kingdom things done. For example, the planet isn't going to sustain itself in this age of hyperindustrialization and hyperconsumption and hyperindividuality unless people responsibly manage carbon emissions and other environmental threats. That was always the plan; this isn't a last-ditch effort. That's what God had in mind from Genesis on.

Have you ever noticed how we naturally work for things we want? We work like crazy to get a promotion, more money, or a hot date. We don't leave those things to work themselves out naturally. We instinctively know that we don't gain traction in important areas unless we set to work with a mission-focused mind-set.

On the other hand, we are too easily deluded when it comes to praying for things that we don't intend to work for, things like whirled peas or world peace. Religious people offer the advice, "Let's just pray about it." Well, how about "Let's get to work on it"?

The workaholic father prays that God will take care of his family while he spends another late night at the office. The free-spending American prays, "God, help those in the world who are hungry tonight." Here's an idea: instead of praying about those things, why don't you work at those things? If your family is going to thrive, it will be because you work less at your job and work more at building intimacy at home. If poor people are going to get fed, it's going to be because you spend less on clothes that will clutter your closet and more on food that will go in hungry mouths.

By the same token, the things you're working on should also be prayed over. Pray about the presentation you have tomorrow as you diligently prepare it. Pray for wisdom about how to discipline your annoying kid—and don't hesitate to ask the advice of others you trust. Pray for supernatural comfort for your hurting friend while at the same time offering hugs of affirmation and sending notes of encouragement—without including any insensitive words of instruction.

We need to pray about the things we are working at, and we need to work at the things we are praying about.

Mission is the seat of our life. It's the platform we sit on. Actually, it's the platform we stand on. Mission is the thing that holds our Revolution together and gives purpose and excitement to reading the Bible, praying, and experiencing community. You weren't put on the planet just to sit in little solemn circles and sing "Jesus Loves Me." You were put here for a purpose. You were put here to work a mission.

And while you're working at your mission, know that a part of God's mission is to work for you. You have a Hero—Someone who has rescued you, redeemed your life, and loves you into wholeness. The most generous thing ever done was God giving the life of His Son for your life. Don't take your eyes off Jesus. Don't forget how much you matter to God.

SPEAKING OF GENEROSITY, WILLINGLY releasing money for Kingdom work is a significant battlefront for followers of Jesus, one that you have to get clued in on.

Jesus talked more about money and possessions than anything else. The Bible says that money is the root of all sorts of evil. Money is behind much of what is wrong with the world: slavery, greed, envy, materialism, cheating. It's also the front of so much of the Kingdom battle. We tend to love money more than we love God, and that is why Jesus was so diligent about bringing this issue to our attention. Money is God's primary competitor for your heart. So for the follower of Christ, financial giving isn't just a way to fund a specific mission; it's funding your spiritual growth, because every time you release money in large quantities, you release the power that the world's system has over you.

What does being generous look like? Well, you're not generous until you can identify something that you don't have and that you could have or that you want to have, but instead you give that money to fund the Revolution. For the minimum-wage worker, that might mean giving up cable TV in order to funnel that money elsewhere. For the millionaire, that might mean choosing not to buy another vacation home so that kids can live in an orphanage. It isn't about not having nice things. You can have nice things but nice things can't have you. It is about regularly releasing the hold money has over you, because whatever you give away doesn't own you.

Every time people come into Crossroads—whether they're an annual auditor or a new attendee who wants to look at our books— they assume they'll uncover a phantom fat cat donor, someone who writes enormous checks every year. But that's not the case. Instead, it's the disciplined, financial generosity of average folks around Crossroads that funds the corner of the Revolution that we are responsible for. And what happens to these generous people? They grow closer to God because they knock out the possibility of money controlling their lives. They've chosen the Kingdom over the world. And, on the other end of it, tangible things happen because of their generosity—things that change the world.

MISSION: SOUTH AFRICA

Several years ago I was at a conference in another city, and I bumped into a pastor from South Africa. His name is Titus Sithole, and we quickly became friends. Titus has taught me incredible things. Long before Bono and the American media got hold of the story, Titus taught me what AIDS was doing to his country. Titus taught me how to operate by faith when you don't have the power of the American dollar. He taught me how to literally have joy in all circumstances.

Titus mentioned that his church, Charity and Faith Mission, had a building that needed a roof. As the leader of a growing American church, I was uniquely positioned to release funds to build that roof, even though our church was still renting space. What ensued was an equal partnership between our churches. Those of us in Cincinnati contributed things the South Africans didn't have, things like money and volunteers. The South Africans returned the favor by contributing to us things that we had very little of—faith and a better understanding of the power of prayer.

One day Titus offered me the opportunity to partner with his church again. They had a vision: they wanted to build the largest privately funded AIDS hospice in South Africa. We were in the middle of raising money for an expansion of our own facility as well as a couple other projects. But we decided to take on the responsibility of funding Charity and Faith Mission's project.

Before allocating any money toward our facility, we committed to build their hospice.

Eighteen months after my verbal commitment to fund the building, I made the twenty-four-hour flight to Johannesburg to be there for the dedication of the hospice. As our driver took us from the airport to the township of Mamelodi, it was as if we were taking a car ride into hell. A South African township represents apartheid at its worst. Originally, the townships were supposed to be only temporary housing for the cheap laborers who would make white mine owners and industrialists rich. But now, decades after the official end of apartheid, the townships remain a fixture of South African society. Their extreme poverty is a stark reminder of the scarring from apartheid that still remains. In some parts of the townships, a hundred thousand people live in plywood shacks with no running water; once a day, a member of each household walks or pushes a wheelbarrow to fill a jug of water.

White people still don't go into the townships, much less live there. On the way to the church, I passed graffiti-walled stores that had shut down. Makeshift businesses dotted the side of the road—women cutting hair in the open air or men lying on the dirt welding a makeshift muffler onto a rundown car. After passing seemingly endless small, rough, outmoded structures, we turned a bend into a driveway. There stood a building that looked totally out of place. It was a beautiful brick structure with a tiled roof. It had two floors and the only elevator in the entire township of one million people. Around the building dozens of people were scrambling to put the finishing touches on the grounds for the next day's festivities.

I sat in the backseat of the van and cried like I did the day I lost Magnum. This was a place of beauty—a place that was going to extend the lives of people dying a painful death from today's plague. A place where wives who got HIV from their cheating husbands would know that someone would care for them. Children who were born with the virus would know that their Father in heaven has compassion on them. Men and women who brought the disease on themselves would know that there is a God who gives grace.

The thing that kept going through my mind—and still does to this day—was that all of this started with a simple yes. A yes to having a friend in Titus. A yes to putting on a roof. And a yes to building a building that had never been built before.

From start to finish, the hospice was the vision of the Charity and Faith Mission. They are the heroes of this story, not those of us in Cincinnati who gave out of our abundance. In South Africa, for a black church to accomplish a project like this would be similar to the homeless building a hospital in America. In human terms, it just doesn't happen. But then again, the Revolution isn't a human endeavor. It operates by faith and by a Power that we cannot see.

Maybe the story of the hospice sounds like an extreme example, something way out of your ballpark. But it really isn't. God is constantly doing very big things with very ordinary people. The key is to be ready and attentive to opportunities that God puts in your life.

MISSION: NEXT DOOR

I don't mean to give you the idea that your mission is something to be found halfway around the world. Your mission is to be a part of the Revolution as it continues to grow, no matter where that is. The vast majority of the work God has for you is probably going to happen right where you live.

Consider the guy down the street who sits on his porch all day. Give him company; make him laugh. What about the mother who never has time to be alone? Go watch her kids for a few hours. Cook a meal for someone. Sit down with a guy who's trying to get a job, and go over his résumé. Give someone exactly what he or she needs.

I want to give you some advice that could be the opposite advice you may be getting from well-meaning "veteran Christians": now that you have become a Christ-follower, don't ditch all your old friends. Experience and history shows that within six months of giving their life to Christ, 90 percent of all Christians have no significant friendships with people who don't know Christ. I'm surprised the number is that low. Every Christ-follower has unbelieving neighbors or unbelieving co-workers. But I know very few who have dinner parties with unbelieving neighbors. I know very few who instigate a cup of coffee or a beer after work with a co-worker who doesn't know Jesus.

It's true that some of your old friends may not be in support of your decision to follow Jesus. Nobody likes losing a drinking buddy. There is tension and an adjustment period in relating to your friends as you undergo spiritual transformation. Your friends may be threatened by your new spiritual fortitude. Many of the key habits of those relationships are like pins that held it together. You may find that Christ starts pulling those pins out of your life because they were sins that He wants to eliminate. As a result, some of your old friendships may begin to fall apart. But as far as it depends on you, stay in those friendships, even though some of them may have to change.

In the movie *I Am Sam*, Sean Penn plays the role of a developmentally disabled father who is fighting to keep custody of his seven-year-old daughter. He hires a lawyer who goes on a personal crusade to preserve his rights as a father. But it's not an easy task; there's not a lot of courtroom evidence to bolster their case that Sam is a capable father. The only people who know Sam well enough to testify on his behalf are his mentally disabled friends. Sam has witnesses, but according to his attorney, they're not "credible" witnesses.

Jesus is calling all of His people to go out into the cities and states in America and to other countries to tell people about the love and power of God. We are to be credible witnesses of what we have seen God do. We need to be able to personally vouch for the power of the Holy Spirit because it has grown our hearts. If we are going to be taken seriously, we've got to be credible.

You'll hear complaints that Christians are misperceived, disrespected, and even bashed. If so, it's not primarily because of a Hollywood bias. It's not primarily because of organizations like the ACLU. It isn't primarily because of conspiracies or dark spiritual forces working to thwart God's plan. All of those things might be true to a degree, but none of them is the real problem.

The real problem is that very few unbelievers ever spend any time with a credible witness for our faith. Very few people have seen with their own eyes what happens when God gets involved in a person's life. They see plenty of witnesses who aren't credible. Just turn on a Christian television station. Would you really believe any of those people? I wouldn't put most of those people on the witness stand to testify the truth of Jesus' power to any of my disconnected friends.

Turn on secular news programs where they debate issues. You'll often find people who represent the "conservative Christian" view, but they usually aren't credible. They look really different than the average guy. They sound different. And, on top of that, the way they respond to questions says to anyone who might be listening, "I'm out of touch, and so is anybody who believes the Bible."

Do you know why Christians appear to be out of touch? Because we are out of touch. We are out of touch with normal people who don't know Jesus. If you aren't around them and they aren't your friends, how can you be in touch with them? How can you be a powerful and credible witness to God's power?

Consider one of the accusations that the religious elite threw at Jesus:

> The Son of Man came eating and drinking, and they say, "Here is a glutton and a drunkard, a friend of tax collectors and 'sinners.'" But wisdom is proved right by her actions.[2]

Jesus was a friend of sinners—a friend of people who didn't have a relationship with God, a friend of normal people. People saw Him spending time with those who weren't morally pristine and Scripturally correct. When the religious elite saw Him with that rough crowd, they dismissed Him as an unspiritual person.

But Jesus didn't deny the charge that He was a friend of tax collectors and sinners. In fact, He took pride in it. "Wisdom is proved right by her actions," He said. In other words, the fruit of His life proved that the way He was doing things was the way things ought to be done.

How sad it is that so few tenured churchgoers can be described as a "friend of sinners." We have sinned grievously against God when people can't accuse us of this. What people saw in Jesus' life they need to see in our lives too. That means being rooted to the real world with real people and trying to really make a difference by bringing them into the Revolution.

---

2. Matthew 11:19

YOU AREN'T GOD'S SALESPERSON

I need to make one thing clear: being a credible witness isn't the same thing as being a salesperson. You may have known people who seem always to be accosting friends, family, and even strangers in hopes of "saving the lost" or "winning souls." One of the problems with this language is the witness's mistaken assumption that he or she is God's salesperson, responsible for getting others to buy in or sign on.

We don't enlist God; He enlists us. When we come into the Kingdom of God, it is because of His work. Therefore, we aren't responsible for getting our friends to become Christ-followers. This is a common albeit innocent mistake. It has led many well-intentioned fresh followers of Christ to actually do damage to others.

> For it is by grace you have been saved, through faith—and this not from yourselves, it is the gift of God—not by works, so that no one can boast. For we are God's workmanship, created in Christ Jesus to do good works, which God prepared in advance for us to do.[3]

This passage makes it clear that our faith isn't something we have earned. Nor is it something we have figured out. Gifts are things that are given that have not been expected or sought after. If the truth of Christ were something we figured out on our own, perhaps we could boast about it. In fact, some people mistakenly do. They look down on those who haven't figured out that Jesus is "the way and the truth and the life."[4] They subtly pat themselves

---

3. Ephesians 2:8–10
4. John 14:6

on the back for doing their homework, counting the cost, and making a bold decision.

To be clear, we are responsible. We do need to do our homework, count the cost, and make a decision. But prior to that happening, God sought us and gave us the desire to do those things. It is God who first seeks us and prompts us to seek. It is Jesus who knocks on our hearts.[5] Then we respond by receiving and then naturally doing the good works that He has prepared us to do.

There's a huge tension here between God's work and our own. There are some people who have spiritually abused others while mistakenly assuming that they have to be God's "Gold Circle Salespeople." Then there are others who excuse themselves from any responsibility for expanding the Revolution on the grounds that God is going to do the work. Theologians and Bible geeks can debate for hours on end about God's role versus our role. The fact of the matter is that we are commanded to be like Jesus, and that includes being a friend of sinners. This is why He commanded His followers to go into the world and be a credible witness to His message of love and forgiveness.

BE A CREDIBLE WITNESS

But how, exactly, do you become a credible witness? You have authentic character, you stay in touch with what's happening in the world, and you clearly communicate the Kingdom by living it out.

HAVE AUTHENTIC CHARACTER

Having authentic character means being real and honest about who you are. It means you aren't putting on an act. When people

---

5. Revelation 3:20

see you for who you are, they see a person of character. And a person of character is a credible witness.

If, for instance, Christians who are in the limelight would do more proactive confession, the cause of Jesus would advance much more quickly. The only time the world sees a Christian confess is when he or she is cornered and has no way out. It's one thing for a pastor to confess that he has sinned after he has been caught in an adulterous affair. It is something much different and more powerful if he confesses before any public scandal that he is a red-blooded male who is trying to figure out how to rein in his sexual passions. It isn't a positive thing for a man to have misguided sexual passions, but it is inherently godly when we voluntarily talk about those in an authentic way.

The apostle Paul was open about his issues when he said things like, "I don't do the things I want to do, and I do the things I don't want to do."[6] This was part of the power of his ministry: honest living.

While you need to be real, you also need to be really growing. Since growth is natural, people should be seeing changes in your character that leave them asking, "What is going on in that person's life? That's a different person than I used to know." The worst thing you could say to me is, "You haven't changed a bit." It means that I have exercised no self-discipline and that God hasn't been involved in my life. It is change in character that gets people to notice the power of God. You would be well advised not to go about advertising your commitment to Christ until you have a character to match it.

A few years ago, a man named Paul started coming to our church. He was a nationally recognized expert on tax law, very

---

6. Romans 7:19, paraphrase

sharp when it came to handling evidence and making a case. He liked what he saw in the church service; he could see that we were a church that was passionate about being inclusive and bringing people into the family of God. But being an agnostic, he knew he had a lot of hurdles to leap before he could embrace the idea of God, let alone receive Jesus and make the changes that the Bible demands of Christ's followers. He decided to sign up for a "Seeker Small Group" and ask his questions and do his homework in a safe environment.

The first night, the others in the group noticed his leg bouncing nervously throughout the meeting. This was new and challenging territory for him, but he knew that he owed it to himself to investigate the claims of the Bible in a diligent manner. Over the course of the next year, he came to embrace Jesus.

He naturally turned his attention to his wife, Courtney. She wasn't an agnostic; rather, she believed that all gods were the same and that it didn't matter which one you believed in. Out of concern for his wife's eternal welfare, Paul asked me, "What should I do to help Courtney become a Christian? Are there any materials you would recommend for a person such as her?"

Paul was a law expert, you see. He wanted to present her with written evidence and make a case. So he wasn't thrilled by my answer. "Paul," I said, "love and serve your wife like Jesus loved and served the church. Jesus died for us, and He tells us men to die for our wives. Don't be concerned about giving her any information at this point. Instead, let her see the transformation that Jesus is doing in your life. When she sees changes taking place in your character, that will be the foundation to words."

That's a slower path than the paper trail Paul was looking for. Character takes time. And serving—well, there just isn't a lot of glory in that. Nevertheless, Paul embarked on the plan of letting his life show his wife who Jesus was. One year later, Courtney was baptized as a new Christ-follower.

A life transformed is evidence of a power that cannot be explained away.

In a recent staff meeting, which is one of the intentional friendship communities that I move in and through, I said some things that came from a judgmental heart toward other churches. Not only was what I said ill-informed and wrong, but my heart was dead wrong in coming to my conclusion.

Margie, a fellow staff member (but more importantly a fellow sister in Christ) lovingly and directly challenged me on why I said what I said. As a revolutionary, she saw that the revolution inside of me had stalled. My immediate response was to repent. This meant telling Margie and the entire staff that I was sorry. Have you ever sent an email to a bunch of people with the subject line being, "My Sin"? You should try it sometime. It cleanses and causes your relationships to be better.

STAY IN TOUCH

The Mississippi flood of '93 was one of the greatest natural disasters our country has ever seen. In order to keep the losses from becoming even more severe, the Army Corps of Engineers strategically put holes in levies upstream from St. Louis to ease the pressure on the mighty concrete floodwalls. If those walls broke, an entire densely populated city would be wiped out.

The trade-off of this plan was that miles of fertile farmland and a few farmhouses would be flooded. Many farmers were not happy. I remember watching a documentary where one farmer who had had his land flooded said, "They didn't care about us. And as far as the people in St. Louis, to hell with them."

This is the kind of attitude many churchgoers unintentionally adopt: "Why should I care about all those people. I don't know them anyway." Whenever we adopt an attitude that says, "My comfort is more important than other people's welfare," we have at that moment taken ourselves off God's playing field. We are at that moment exhibiting a selfishness that is of the world and not of the Kingdom. What would have happened had Jesus said to His Father, "Why would You put Me on the cross? You don't care about Me! As far as the sinners in the world, they can all end up in hell as far as I'm concerned."

When a Christ-follower stays inside the safe walls of a church, Christian school, or holy huddle and refuses to venture out into a world estranged from God and flooded by sin, that person is acting selfishly and unbiblically. Jesus told us to be salt and light:

> You are the salt of the earth. But if the salt loses its saltiness, how can it be made salty again? It is no longer good for anything, except to be thrown out and trampled by men.
>
> You are the light of the world. A city on a hill cannot be hidden. Neither do people light a lamp and put it under a bowl. Instead they put it on its stand, and it gives light to everyone in the house. In the same way, let your light shine before men, that they may see your good deeds and praise your Father in heaven.[7]

If a light isn't in the presence of darkness, it isn't doing anybody any good. We've got to make this world a well-lit kind of place. We've got to get people out of the scary darkness, because we know what that darkness can feel like. No dark room has ever been able to beat a candle. So where there is hatred, bring the light

---

7. Matthew 5:13–16

of love. Where there is selfishness, bring the light of generosity. It's how Jesus did it. And the more that selfless kind of love happens, the more robust the Revolution becomes.

CLEAR COMMUNICATION

Jesus wasn't just near people who were outside the Kingdom. He was near them so He could serve them and communicate to them the truth of God. It is not enough for us simply to be around unbelievers. We must be clearly communicating who Jesus is and what the Gospel offers them.

I've heard many people say, "I just let my life be a witness"—and that normally means, "I don't ever talk about my faith or clearly communicate to others why and how to become a Christ-follower." When people say this, they're revealing their ignorance as to what the Bible says about communicating our faith; they're also revealing their fear of being identified as a follower of Jesus. They're afraid of being mocked.

You wouldn't be reading this book right now if someone hadn't clearly communicated to you how to be a Christ-follower. I've never had somebody come up to me and say, "Brian, I notice that you don't use many four-letter words and that you return your rented movies on time and that you don't mix your recyclables. You obviously walk with God. How can I become part of the Kingdom?"

Instead, when a genuine friendship has been built, a friend comes to a point in life where he or she is open to spiritual things. Then you can communicate God's truth about that person's need and Jesus' offer of wholeness. At some point, we must clearly communicate who God is, what He offers and expects of us human beings, and how to become a part of His family. People can respect what you say when your life doesn't completely contradict what's coming out of your mouth. I don't mean you have to be perfect, but I do mean you have to show a commitment to live God's way and a willingness to accept responsibility when you mess up.

For clear communication to happen, you must know three things: the moment to speak, your own story, and the basics.

KNOWING THE MOMENT

"The moment" is that time when you get an opportunity to share what your relationship with God is all about. I'm not a fan of door-to-door evangelism. I don't like handing out weird and scary religious tracts in the men's public bathroom. I don't like anything that is forced and prepackaged. Standard mass-communication methods fail to recognize that every person is a unique creation of God and that God is doing something unique in him or her.

And don't give me your prepackaged spiel when we haven't established a relationship with each other. I'm angered when someone does that to me, even when I agree with what the person is saying. It bothers me so much that I'll object to something that they don't know the answer to, just to jack them up.

As a communicator, I tend to not use the word evangelism because it lacks clarity in modern times. Though it is found in the Bible and is a mandate for all Christians, the term has accumulated a lot of baggage that's foreign to the Bible. Too many people who speak of evangelism are trying to promote a strategy that involves minimal friendship, even false friendship. If those methods ever truly worked, they certainly don't work now. Today, evangelism requires credibility, which only comes from a relationship.

There will come a moment in your relationships when the opportunity to talk about your faith will present itself. You'll sense this moment and then open your mouth and begin that clear communication—though clear doesn't mean perfect. You don't have to spew out a memorized spiritual formula on how not to go to hell. Not only is that ineffective, but we are hoping our friends get engaged in the kingdom—which is about much more than not going to hell. And that moment is any time you think your friend will be receptive to hearing, any time when you can spend a few uninterrupted minutes talking about something that is close to your heart.

There are limitless scenarios when the moment might occur, but two common scenarios are a time of crisis and a time of unusual questioning of what life is all about. In times of crisis, people realize they aren't in control. They realize that they aren't God—and that they need the God who is. Your moment probably won't be in the receiving line at the funeral, but perhaps shortly thereafter. On the other hand, often when people get something they've always wanted, they realize they don't feel the way they always wanted to feel. If they verbalize something of this nature, be prepared to talk about what life is all about.

KNOWING YOUR STORY

Nothing communicates more powerfully than a person's story. You might hear people use the traditional word "testimony" to refer to that story.

A testimony is what you say from the witness stand to communicate what has happened in your life as a result of Jesus' power. I highly encourage you to take the time to write your story out on paper. The process of organizing your thoughts will enable you to communicate very clearly, and you'll be able to share it with greater ease. Though you will modify key points of your story in sensitivity to the moment and to the person with whom you are communicating, 90 percent of what you say will not change. Writing your story down will give you some extra confidence.

> **Testimony:** a verbal articulation of what Jesus has done in your life.

Every story should have three sections: the past, the point, and the present. The past is what your life was like prior to having a relationship with Jesus. The point is what was involved in your turning point from serving yourself to serving God. The present is the tangible difference God has made in your life.

ALLIES, NOT AFFILIATES

All across God's Kingdom are people who are parked in churches. I call them "garage Christians." They believe that because they're in church then they are Christians. Being in a church doesn't make you a Christ-follower any more than being in a garage makes you a car. Regardless of where they are, their demeanor doesn't say they're in the Kingdom. Being a churchgoer makes you a Christian only in the sense that you are affiliating yourself with the Christian religion as opposed to being affiliated with Islam or Mormonism.

But God doesn't want affiliates. He wants allies. He wants people who are in relationship with Him, not people connected to a religion. He wants people who are fellow fighters for His agenda as opposed to loose associates. Bringing people into His family is a key part of God's agenda. The joy of working on God's agenda and working to honor Him is a thrill that mature Christ-followers can't live without.

That is why I have a group of people whom I am praying for, strategizing about, and working to bring into the Revolution. These people go onto my "Paste List." It's a list of names I stick on my bathroom mirror. As I put toothpaste on my toothbrush and work away the potential cavities, I ask God to bless these friends of mine. I pray for their families, their jobs, and, most importantly, their hearts.

Awhile back I came home from a dinner with Libby and three other couples. It was an incredible night. Libby and I both remarked on how much fun we had. We weren't sure if it was because we needed a night away from the normal routine of life, because the dining experience was so good, or because these friends were not churchy types who tried to impress us with their spirituality. Their realness was refreshing.

> **Paste List:** contains the names of normal friends and is stuck to the bathroom mirror. You pray for them every time you brush your teeth. Once a person comes to know Jesus, his or her name is crossed off the list, signifying they were "pasted."

Right before I went to bed, I was struck by how thickheaded I was. Staring at me from the top right-hand corner of my mirror were six names on my Paste List. They were the names of the six people Libby and I had just spent the evening with. God had naturally arranged the evening and worked in it—and it hadn't even crossed my mind that this was an "evangelistic" function.

Those people weren't objects of a strategy. They weren't on their way to being notches on my Bible. They were friends whom I love dearly. Since I love them dearly, I can't help but work naturally toward bringing them into a relationship with Jesus. It was so natural that I hadn't realized until that moment in front of my mirror that God was directly answering me.[8]

So right now, look around. Get your head out of this book and see who's sitting near you or which of those people whose number is in your cell phone really need to talk. Look at the woman behind the cash register, the kid next to you in class, the parent whom you've ignored for five years because you can't bring yourself to forgive. Love those people. Serve them, celebrate them, fight for them. Because that's how the Kingdom comes.

---

8. This section of the book was written five years ago. All of these friends have since joined the Revolution.

MISSION:
LETTER FROM A REVOLUTIONARY

I GREW UP WITH AN ANGRY FATHER AND SEVERAL INCIDENTS OF SEXUAL ABUSE, INCLUDING AN AWFUL EXPERIENCE AT MY CHURCH. BUT AFTER MANY YEARS OF DWELLING IN MY OWN ANGER, I STARTED TO UNDERSTAND GOD IN A NEW WAY: AS A GENTLEMAN. I WENT BACK TO THE PLACE WHERE I HAD BEEN ABUSED IN THE CHURCH, YELLED AND PRAYED TO GOD, AND EVENTUALLY LET HIS GRACE HEAL ME.

AFTER MY OWN HEALING AND RENEWED CONNECTION WITH GOD, I WANTED TO REACH OUT IN MY OWN NEIGHBORHOOD, WHICH IS THE HUB OF THE CITY'S GAY COMMUNITY. AFTER READING *BLUE LIKE JAZZ* BY DONALD MILLER (AND HAVING A NEW UNDERSTANDING OF WHAT THE BIBLE WAS SAYING IN STORIES LIKE MARS HILL IN ACTS, WHERE PAUL MET PEOPLE WHERE THEY WERE), I DECIDED THAT I WANTED TO CONNECT WITH MY OWN NEIGHBORHOOD IN THAT WAY.

I DECIDED TO CREATE A CONFESSIONAL TENT AT MY LOCAL GAY PRIDE FESTIVAL. I HAD A GREAT FRIEND THE FIRST YEAR WHO WOULD GENTLY COAX

PEOPLE TO COME IN, AND MY HUSBAND WOULD CARE
FOR PEOPLE AND CHECK IN WITH THEM AS THEY
LEFT. WHEN THEY CAME IN, I WOULD SAY, "THIS IS
A CONFESSIONAL, BUT YOU DON'T HAVE TO CONFESS
TO ME. I WANT TO CONFESS TO YOU. I WANT TO SAY
I'M SORRY IF YOU HAVE EVER BEEN HURT OR FELT
JUDGED BY SOMEONE WHO CALLED HIMSELF OR HER-
SELF A CHRISTIAN. I BELIEVE THAT GOD IS A GOD OF
LOVE, AND I'M SORRY IF YOU HAVE EVER FELT THAT
PAIN OF JUDGMENT." I DID A LOT OF RESEARCH
ABOUT THIS BEFORE I DID IT, AND ULTIMATELY I
FELT THAT THE BIBLE SAID A LOT MORE ABOUT NOT
JUDGING AND ABOUT LOVING THAN IT DID ABOUT
HOMOSEXUALITY. SO I DECIDED THAT, IN THIS ONE
SPACE, I WANTED PEOPLE TO FEEL LOVED AND NOT
JUDGED SO THAT MAYBE THEY COULD BE INSPIRED BY
LOVE, NOT JUDGED OR CONDEMNED INTO CHANGE.
IMMEDIATELY MOST PEOPLE BEGAN TO CRY, AND
SO MANY SHARED THEIR STORIES OF BEING HURT.
I'VE NOW DONE THE TENT THREE YEARS IN A ROW,
AND I COULD FILL A BOOK WITH THE STORIES OF
HEALING. PEOPLE HAVE BEEN ENCOUNTERING
GOD'S LOVE FOR THE FIRST TIME IN THEIR LIVES.

MEANWHILE, GOD HAS CONTINUED TO HEAL ME. THERE IS NOT A SINGLE THING THAT HE HAS LED ME TO SAY THAT HAS NOT ALSO BEEN WHAT I NEEDED TO HEAR. A TRANSVESTITE LOOKED AT ME ONCE AND SAID, "THAT'S ALL WELL AND GOOD, BUT I JUST DON'T BELIEVE THERE'S A GOD." I WANTED TO EXPLAIN HOW THERE WAS A GOD AND I KNEW THERE WAS, AND I WANTED TO QUOTE THE BIBLE, BUT SOMETHING PROMPTED ME TO SAY SIMPLY, "OKAY, BUT YOU ARE NOT A MISTAKE." HE STARTED CRYING IMMEDIATELY, AND SO DID I.

I AM NOT A MISTAKE EITHER, AND GOD HAS POWERFULLY CHANGED MY LIFE THROUGH THE COMMUNITY I HAVE EXPERIENCED AT MY CHURCH, THROUGH HELPING ME TO UNDERSTAND HIS WORD IN NEW WAYS, AND THROUGH DEEP AND LIFE-CHANGING PRAYER.

THE BEGINNING

This book was never intended to give you an ironclad argument for everything we've explored. Nor did it come close to covering everything important to being a Christ-follower. What you've been given is a toolbox that contains things you need in order to grow closer to Jesus as His Kingdom grows closer to fulfillment.

While the three-legged stool analogy is helpful in communicating the importance of having in place the four elements of Bible, prayer, community, and mission, the foundation upon which the stool stands is the work of Jesus. Being a Christ-follower isn't about you—what you deserve or need to earn. It is about Jesus and what He has done for you. His death for you shows that you are of infinite value. The value of any item is what someone is willing to pay for it. Your value, then, is Jesus Himself. God gave the best He had to you, because you are worth it to Him.

> I have been crucified with Christ and I no longer live, but Christ lives in me. The life I live in the body, I live by faith in the Son of God, who loved me and gave himself for me.[1]

---

1. 2 Timothy 2:3–4

When you surrender to Jesus, God doesn't view you as a problem that needs managing. As far as God is concerned, your problems are dead to Him—at least as far as those problems keep you separated from Him. When He looks at you, He sees what is in you: the Holy Spirit. And the Holy Spirit is powerful and pure. Believe this: to God, you are powerful and pure.

THE REVOLUTION IS UNDERWAY, and while it is both exhilarating and fulfilling, it is also messy, chaotic, and unpredictable. The history of warfare tells us that, despite the best-laid plans of commanders, when battle happens, the unpredictable happens as well.

You are a soldier called to war.[2] When Jesus gathered His potential revolutionaries and spoke the Sermon on the Mount, He told them that the Kingdom of God is a war waged with unconventional weapons: praying for our enemies, forgiving and loving the people who hurt us, and living as Jesus lived. Your willingness to pick up these unconventional weapons signals to God that you've fully joined the Revolution, that you'll fight anything that is against God and not driven by love.

But on the battlefield, every soldier will eventually experience what is called the "fog of war." Things that were previously clear suddenly become convoluted. Communication might be cut off. Maybe it becomes hard to get clear directions from the commander, or individual soldiers stop functioning as a team unit and the fighting feels more like a solo show.

Under these conditions, it is imperative that you fulfill the last command you clearly heard from God. Whatever you sense that God wants you to do, you must complete that assignment before

---

2. Psalm 144:1

another one comes along. If you are having sex with someone you aren't married to, there will be a fog in your life until you repent and change. If you are spending all your resources on yourself and not giving generously to others, there will be a fog around other matters you want direction on. Your response to God—the action you take when He speaks truth to you—will communicate how intimately involved in your life He should get.

This is a fresh start. I'm excited for you and for how you'll impact God's Kingdom. I'm even jealous of you, because you don't have to peel away as many false layers of religiosity as I did. To go back and do it all again, understanding the Revolution and what that means, would be incredible. I can't do that, but I can encourage you to enjoy this season of your life. And don't allow anyone to look down on your "youth."[3] Right now, there's probably a simplicity to the way you view things. You see black and white when other longtime followers may only see changing shades of gray. And it's true—things you're now black on will change to white or gray later. But the Kingdom needs your raw passion and simple faith.

You have much to offer in your newness. Don't hold back. We need you.

3. 1 Timothy 4:12

APDX

QUESTIONS YOU MAY BE ASKING

I f you are standing in the bookstore right now, then get ready to be annoyed by the brief answers. These questions are helpful for people who have laid the foundation by reading the previous chapters.

I'm not trying to fully answer any of these questions, but simply to knock down some of the walls that may be keeping you from advancing the Kingdom. In time, you can blow through the wall completely by answering these questions more thoroughly.

I DON'T FEEL ANY DIFFERENT. SHOULDN'T I FEEL SOMETHING?

It is possible that if you don't feel anything different, maybe you haven't received anything different. There is a difference between having beliefs and having the Spirit of God inside of you. If you want to follow Jesus and be a part of the Kingdom, then ask Him for the Holy Spirit right now and yield yourself.

If you still don't "feel" anything, don't worry. I don't feel a lot of what other people say they feel as they follow Christ. Or maybe you have become numb to the love of God that has been on you for a long time. Maybe your ability to feel is something that will change with time. Keep trusting the process—Bible reading, prayer, community, mission—and you will eventually "feel" God.

HOW DO I "HEAR" GOD TALK TO ME?

Learning to hear God's voice is a lifelong process. You'll come to understand with greater clarity the unique dialect that God will use with you. He doesn't speak the same way to all people. You may get dreams. You may get counsel from other people. You may get something that leaps off a page of the Bible. You may sense God's voice while you're in nature, while you're serving, or when you're creating art. Continue to put yourself in places where you come alive, and you'll come to realize that it is because God is meeting you there.

God wants us to recognize His voice, so He'll usually start with small assignments—not with "Pick up and move to Alaska." The assignments might seem small and insignificant, but God does not want us to despise humble beginnings. He will give us small responsibilities to see if He can trust us with bigger responsibilities. If you think you are hearing from God, look for confirmation through prayer, the Bible, and your community. And when you hear Him, remember always to obey Him. That encourages Him to speak to you again.

WHAT ABOUT THE ISSUE OF _____?

In the years ahead, you are going to come up against a lot of tough issues. You are going to have to figure out what God's heart is regarding poverty, the environment, homosexual sex, and the mystery of Jerry Springer. But you now have the tools to explore those and many other issues. Take your time. You are on a journey.

And guess what? Whatever you believe right now, it is likely that you will believe something else later. And it's also possible that you will flip-flop back again. The thing to remember is that it isn't the issue that's the issue. The Person of God is the issue.

DO I NEED TO GIVE UP BEER, CIGARETTES, CUSSING, MOVIES, ETC.?

Give up beer? No. Give up cheesy chick flicks? Absolutely. (This is supposed to be funny. If you don't get that by now, this book is probably driving you crazy.) Jesus wants you to have freedom. You will learn that you are freer when you give up certain things—and some things that other people shouldn't have are fine for you to have. And there are some things that none of us should have and others that all of us should. Sorry . . . Simplistic answers come from religious people, not Jesus.

I STILL DON'T UNDERSTAND WHY JESUS HAD TO DIE FOR MY SINS.

I'm not sure exactly why, either. I mean, God could have concocted any number of different plans, but the one He chose to go with was the most dramatic, intense, and in tune with the history of religions. Ancient religions have often sought to appease the gods with sacrifices. Most of the time it was in crazy ways like sacrificing a virgin or a child. The real God has no part in that.

However, in ancient Israel people would place their hands on a lamb, and the priest would kill the animal. As the blood was draining, the person offering the sacrifice couldn't help but think, *There must be punishment for sin. If I were God, I wouldn't be as patient with others as He is with me.* The death of the animal was a reminder of the grace, mercy, and patience of God who wasn't requiring death of the person who sinned.

When Jesus came, He was hailed as the "Lamb of God, who takes away the sin of the world."[1] The perfect Lamb offered up on a cross for a person God loves very much: you.

---

1. John 1:29

DID JESUS LITERALLY AND HISTORICALLY RISE FROM THE DEAD?

Yes, and there are a number of reasons why it's rational to believe that this actually happened. The importance of the literal and historical resurrection is detailed in 1 Corinthians 15. Also, you may want to read books by Lee Strobel, Gary Habermas, or N. T. Wright for a deep dive.

SHOULD I GET BAPTIZED?

Yes. Read the book of Acts, and you'll see that it is a normal thing to be immersed after you become a Christ-follower. The book of Romans in the Bible says that when we go under the water, we identify with Christ who went into the grave, and when we come up out of the water, we identify with His resurrection. Baptism signifies what has already happened to us spiritually. Our old identity as a sinner is killed, and we rise with a new identity as a holy child of God.

WILL MY FRIENDS WHO DON'T BELIEVE IN JESUS BE IN HEAVEN?

The Bible tells me not to judge. That means it is in God's job description—not mine—to decide and to know certain things. This I do know: after having experienced the freedom that Jesus has given me, I want to enable as many of my friends as possible to receive Him.

THE BIBLE WAS WRITTEN A LONG, LONG TIME AGO. THINGS HAVE CHANGED. AREN'T THERE A LOT OF THINGS TAUGHT AND EVEN COMMANDED IN THE BIBLE THAT AREN'T REALLY APPLICABLE TODAY? WHICH ONES ARE THEY, AND HOW CAN I TELL?

There are a lot of things in the Bible that aren't applicable today. For one, don't kill your dog to atone for your sins. There are other places where Bible scholars disagree about what should still be enforced. Don't be upset about not understanding all this right now. Instead, be excited about the journey of discovery that God has you on. In the meantime, trust that the Holy Spirit will enable you to clearly apply what you need to know and do today.

IS IT TRUE THAT IF I OBEY GOD AND I'M GENEROUS AND I'M NICE TO OTHER PEOPLE, GOD WILL BLESS ME WITH FINANCIAL PROSPERITY AND HAPPINESS?

Maybe. There are verses in the Bible that speak to this. At the same time, there are verses in the Bible that say pain and problems will come to even the most righteous. You'll never go wrong doing the right thing and being a blessing to others. At the same time, there are people in countries around the world who will never be prosperous the way we define it, yet God is blessing them.

OKAY. I DECIDED TO FOLLOW JESUS, BUT HOW CAN I BE SURE IT REALLY TOOK AND I'M GONNA END UP IN HEAVEN, NOT HELL?

The Bible says to "work out your salvation with fear and trembling."[2] It is good to examine where you are. At the same time, it isn't good to be focused on whether or not you have a bus pass to pie in the sky when you die. You can experience God right now. So worry about how yielded to Him you are today, and tomorrow will take care of itself.

I'M TRYING TO FOLLOW JESUS, BUT I KEEP SCREWING UP. WHAT'S UP WITH THAT?

Following Jesus doesn't mean you behave perfectly in every situation. Sometimes you'll say and do stupid things and feel like a screw-up. But becoming like Jesus in your thoughts and actions is a lifelong journey. Luckily, you're not alone. Jesus left the Holy Spirit to help, so try asking Him for help the next time you're worried about screwing up—and for forgiveness when you do.

---

2. Philippians 2:12

... being confident of this, that he who began a good work in you will carry it on to completion until the day of Christ Jesus.[3]

I BELIEVE, AND I'M TRYING REALLY HARD TO DO WHAT GOD TELLS ME, BUT MY LIFE IS SUCKING EVEN MORE NOW THAN BEFORE I KNEW WHO JESUS WAS. SO WHAT'S THE POINT?

This experience isn't too uncommon. We didn't go into much depth in the book, but the fact of the matter is that in a Revolution there are two sides. One side that is about freedom, and the other side is about bondage. Jesus said, "The thief comes only to steal and kill and destroy."[4] Once you switch sides, the thief may try to steal you back. Common tactics include pain, doubt, rejection, and loneliness. This is why it is critical to lean into community. You need people to love on you and tell you that you are in a good place and that God approves of you.

WHY DOESN'T GOD TAKE AWAY MY PAIN OR MY ADDICTION?

Someday He might. But more often what God does is put us in places where we have to lean into Him. Our pain often forces us closer to God, and that closeness brings about a power to kick things that we couldn't kick on our own. God isn't into using a magic wand to eliminate problems.

WHEN I READ THE BIBLE, IT SEEMS LIKE GOD IS TICKED OFF. WHAT'S UP WITH ALL THE SMITING?

In John 14:7 Jesus says, "If you really knew me, you would know my Father as well. From now on, you do know him and have seen him." The predominant key to understanding God's heart and character

---

3. Philippians 1:6
4. John 10:10

is knowing Jesus. He is the lens through which everything should be viewed. Once we understand God's love and endurance—and those are also clearly seen in the Old Testament before Jesus' physical appearance on Earth—then we can begin to realize there is a lot more going on behind the scenes than we may realize.

God isn't in perpetual-anger mode. However, we have screwed up His world and ignored Him. Wouldn't you be ticked too? In fact, you would undoubtedly behave far worse than we accuse God of behaving.

WHERE IS GOD IN WAR, WHEN NATURAL DISASTERS LIKE TSUNAMIS AND HURRICANES STRIKE, AND WHEN CHILDREN ARE TERMINALLY ILL?

God is hoping you are going to do something about the situation. That is what the Revolution is about and why you are here. We can't ask God for freedom but not want any downsides to that freedom. The things that aren't right in the world are both a result of people abusing their freedom and signs that the planet is out of control. We need to use our freedom to come closer to Jesus and then rely on His power as we engage our world with love.

WHY DOESN'T GOD MORE DIRECTLY INTERVENE TO STOP THINGS LIKE PAIN, TURMOIL, ABUSE, OR THE LOSS OF A CHILD?

God may directly intervene far more than we realize. Who knows what other awful things would happen were God to fully remove His hand from our world? But know that all painful things cause God pain as well. There is nothing that we feel that He hasn't felt. He has been through the worst of it, including losing a Child—a Child who never did anything wrong, who always loved perfectly, yet was tortured, abused, and killed. God's been there.